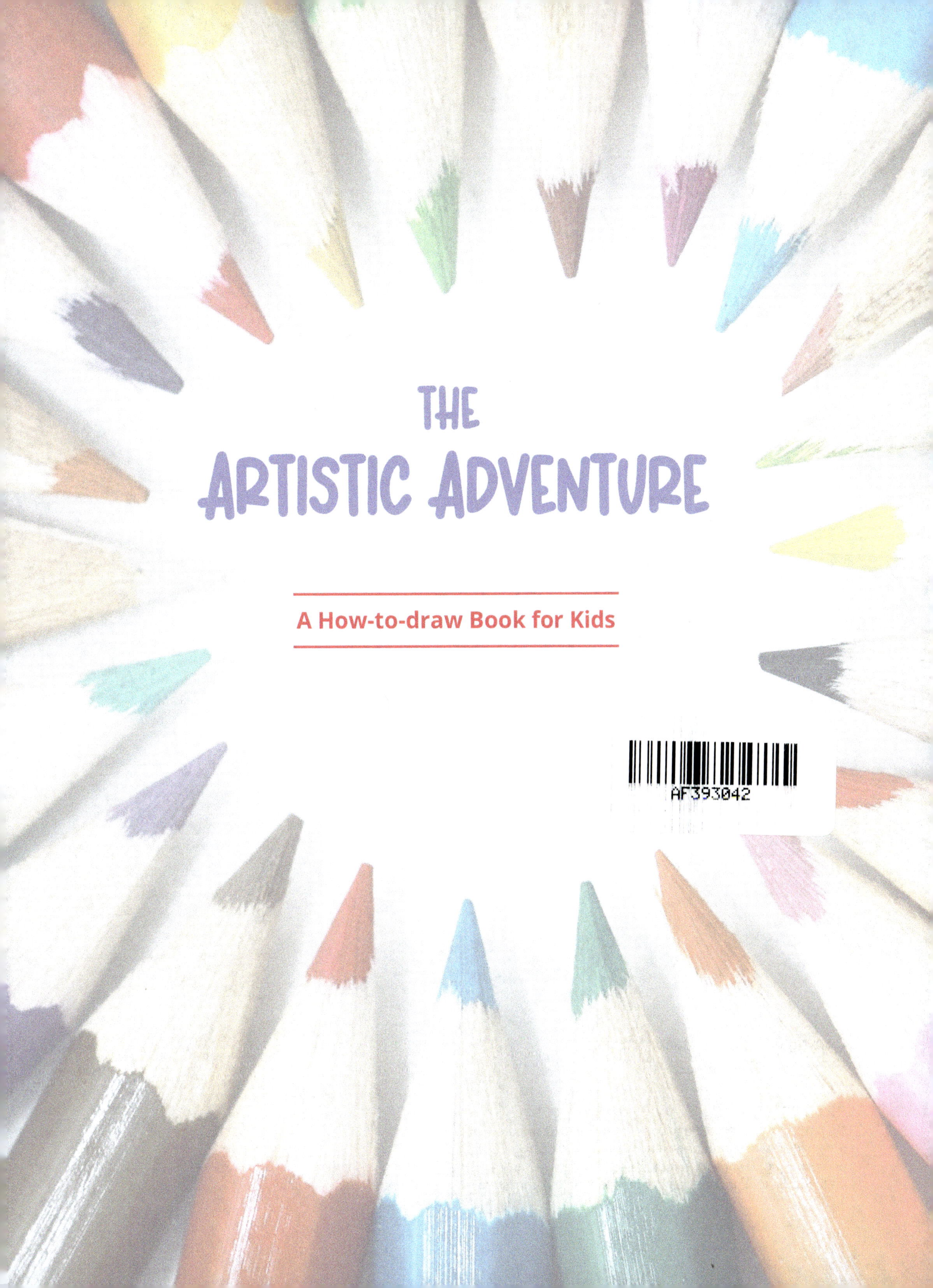

THE
ARTISTIC ADVENTURE
A How-to-draw Book for Kids
AF393042

HEY THERE!

Hello there, budding artist! Are you ready to embark on an amazing drawing adventure? Get your pencils and your imagination ready because we're about to dive into the colorful world of drawing.

Welcome to "Let's Draw and Have Fun!". This book is perfect for creative spirits like yourself. It doesn't matter if you're a beginner or an aspiring Picasso because this book will help you unlock your artistic superpowers and help you bring your drawings to life.

But hey, let's not get too serious here. The most important thing about art is to have fun with it. We're going to keep things casual, fun, and full of laughs! Drawing is about expressing yourself and having a good time along the way, after all.

Now, you might be wondering, "What is so cool about drawing?" Well, dear artist, drawing is like magic! With a simple stroke of your pencil, you can create worlds, make animals come to life, and even design your own superhero with an amazing cape. Isn't that awesome?

And guess what? Drawing is not just about making pretty pictures. It's a superpower that helps you observe the world around you and express your feelings and ideas. Want to show happiness? Draw a big, smiley sun! Feeling a bit mischievous? Sketch a cheeky monkey swinging from a tree! The possibilities are endless.

Throughout this book, we'll explore everything from drawing friendly animals and cool characters to amazing landscapes and everyday objects. We'll learn the secrets of perspective, discover the wonders of color, and find out how to make our artwork truly unique.

But hold on tight, because we're not just going to teach you how to draw. We're also going to warm up those creative muscles with fun exercises, tell silly jokes along the way, and encourage you to let your imagination soar high, like a rocket.

Remember, there are no "mistakes" in art—only happy accidents and opportunities to try new things. So, embrace your inner artist, be patient with yourself, and most importantly, have a ton of fun!

So, are you ready? Let's dive into the colorful world of drawing and have a blast!

DRAWING TOOLS

Welcome to the first chapter of our fantastic drawing adventure. Before we jump into the exciting world of drawing, let's get to know our trusty tools that will help us bring our imaginations to life!

PENCILS

Our best buddies on this artistic journey are pencils. They come in different sizes and hardness. Just like Goldilocks, we need to find the one that's "just right" for us. Try different pencils and see which one feels comfy in your hand. Remember, pencils love to dance on paper, so hold them gently and let them glide!

ERASERS

Oops, made a little slip-up? No worries! That's where erasers come to the rescue! They're like magical wands that can whisk away any unwanted lines. Erasers are our secret weapons to fix any little "oopsies" and make our drawings look even more amazing!

PAPER

Now, let's talk about the magical land where our drawings come to life —paper! You can use any kind of paper, but drawing paper is extra special. It's smooth and makes your pencil lines look super sharp. Plus, it loves to soak up all the colors and ideas from your imagination!

COLORING TOOLS

Drawing is not just about pencils and lines; it's also about splashing colors all around! Crayons, markers, and colored pencils are like a rainbow in your hand. Experiment with different colors, mix them up, and create your own magical hues. Remember, there are no "right" or "wrong" colors—just the ones that make you smile!

RULERS

Meet our straight-line superheroes—rulers! They help us draw perfectly straight lines and create neat shapes. But be careful, because rulers can be a bit sneaky. Make sure to hold them steady when you're using them. You don't want wobbly lines or runaway shapes, do you?

Don't worry if things don't look perfect right away. Drawing takes practice, just like riding a bike or making the perfect pancake. With a little bit of patience and a whole lot of giggles, you'll be amazed at what you can create!

So, get those pencils sharpened, put on your drawing capes, and let's dive into the colorful world of art together. Ready, set, draw!

TEST PAGE

In this book you'll find several exercises that you can do directly in the book or on a separate sheet. If you choose to do them in this book we recommend testing your material first on this page. There's nothing worse than creating a beautiful drawing only to find that your markers have bled through the page to whatever masterpiece you drew on the next page.

TEST PAGE

UNDERSTANDING LINES, SHAPES AND FORMS

It's time to dive into the wonderful world of lines, shapes, and forms. These are like the building blocks of our drawings, the secret ingredients that make our artwork extra special. So, let's grab our pencils and get ready to explore!

everything you want to draw, whether it's a cute puppy or a tall tree, can be simplified into shapes. Imagine that! Learning about shapes helps us understand the world around us and make our drawings even more awesome. By breaking down objects into simple circles, squares, and triangles, we can easily bring them to life on paper.

You have probably already seen this in real life many times before if you've ever played with building blocks.

You can clearly see that both images are locomotives, yet the second one is made up of basic shapes. Let's take it a step further shall we...

Get ready for some fun, little artists! We're going to dive into exciting exercises that will help us become masters of lines, shapes, and forms. These exercises are like mini adventures that will strengthen our drawing skills and boost our creativity. We'll doodle, scribble, and sketch! So, grab your pencils and get ready to warm up those artistic muscles. Remember, these exercises are not about being perfect, but about having a blast and exploring the endless possibilities of drawing. Get ready to unleash your imagination and let the magic begin!

LINES

Lines are like magical trails that guide our drawings. They can be straight as a ruler or wiggly like a snake. They can be long, short, thick, or thin. Let's practice drawing different lines together! Try drawing a wavy line that looks like a roller coaster or a zigzag line that jumps around like a lightning bolt. Be as creative as you can!

TRACE THE LINES

TRACE THE LINES

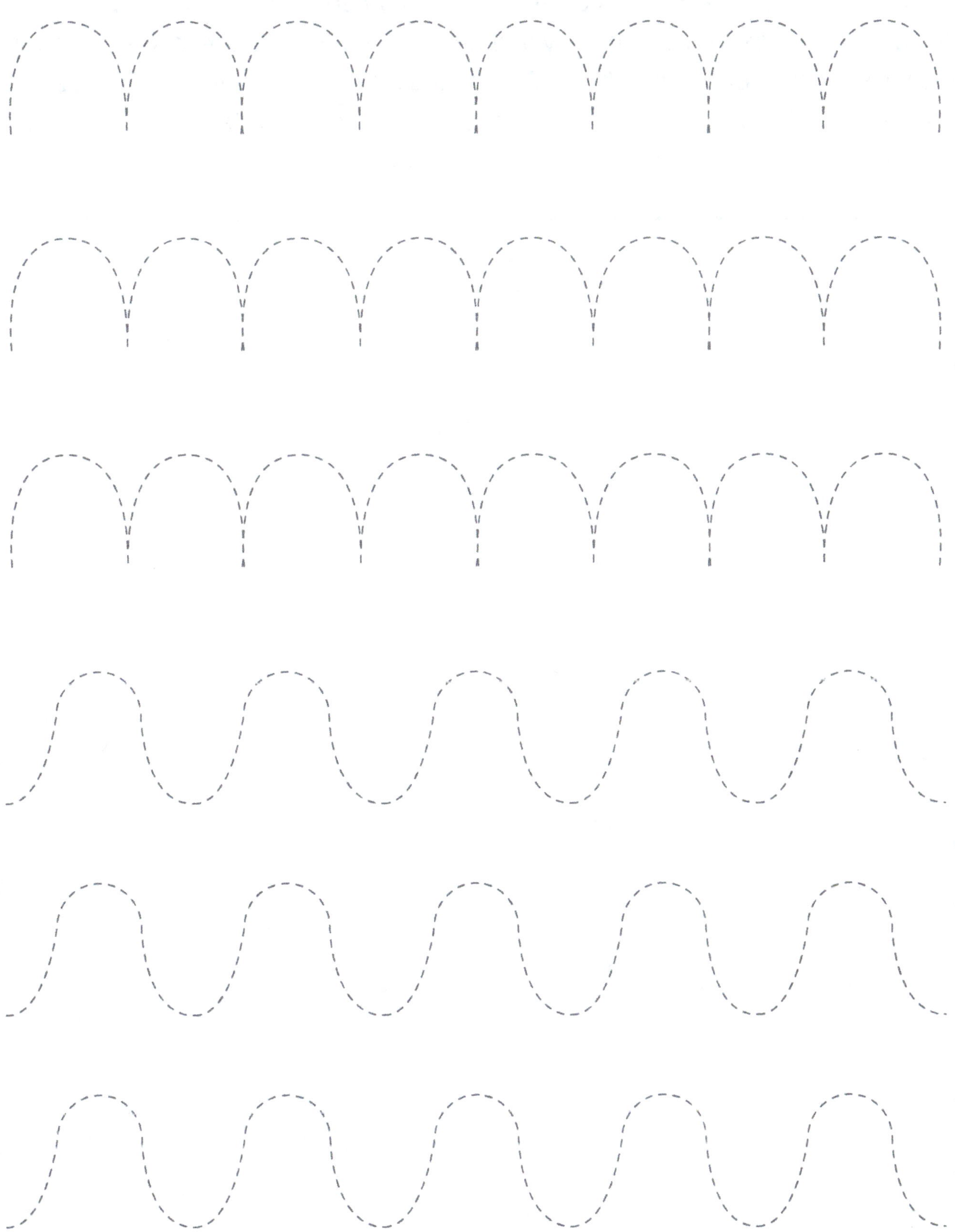

SHAPES

Shapes are the superheroes of drawing. They can be round like a ball, square like a box, or even pointy like a triangle. Let's discover the amazing things we can create with shapes! Draw a circle and add eyes, a nose, and a big smile. Voila! You've just created a friendly sun. Now, let's draw a square and add windows and a door. It's a cozy house!

TRACE THE SHAPES

TRACE THE SHAPES

FORMS

Now, let's add some magic to our drawings with forms. Forms are like shapes that come to life, as if they jumped right out of the page! Imagine a cube with six sides, or a cylinder that looks like a tall can. Let's draw a cube and make it look like a yummy gift box. Don't forget to add a bow on top!

TRACE THE SHAPES

TRACE THE SHAPES

By understanding lines, shapes, and forms, we can bring our drawings to a whole new level of awesomeness. Remember, there's no limit to your imagination! You can create anything you dream of, from friendly animals to cool spaceships.

So, keep those pencils dancing, experiment with lines and shapes, and let your creativity soar high! Drawing is all about having fun, exploring, and letting your imagination shine.

THE IMPORTANCE OF OBSERVATION

Hey there, little artists with eagle eyes! In this chapter, we're going to discover the superpower of observation. You know what? The world around us is filled with fascinating things just waiting to be turned into incredible drawings. But to capture their magic, we need to become keen observers.

Observation is like a superpower for artists because it helps us truly understand the world around us. When we observe closely, we notice all the little details—the way light casts shadows, the curves and angles of objects, and the colors that bring them to life. By observing, we train our eyes and our minds to see things as they truly are, allowing us to capture their essence in our drawings. It's like having a special lens that helps us create realistic and captivating artwork. So, get ready to sharpen your observation skills because they hold the key to unlocking your artistic potential!

So, put on your detective hats, grab your magnifying glasses, and let's embark on an adventure of observation!

PAY ATTENTION

Observation starts with paying attention to the details. Look closely at the objects around you—their shapes, colors, and textures. Let's practice by observing a flower. Notice its petals, how they curl and overlap. Look at the colors, the delicate lines, and the center of the flower. Can you see the tiny pollen? Amazing, isn't it?

WRITE A DETAILED DESCRIPTION OF YOUR SURROUNDINGS

EXPLORING NATURE

Nature is a treasure trove of wonders just waiting to be observed and drawn. Take a nature walk and see what catches your eye—colorful leaves, chirping birds, or swirling clouds. Observe how trees stretch towards the sky, how the wind rustles the grass, and how waves crash against the shore. Nature is the best teacher when it comes to observing the beauty around us!

Nature is a treasure trove of wonders just waiting to be observed and drawn. Take a nature walk and see what catches your eye—colorful leaves, chirping birds, or swirling clouds. Observe how trees stretch towards the sky, how the wind rustles the grass, and how waves crash against the shore. Nature is the best teacher when it comes to observing the beauty around us!

Go outside and find some things in nature that you can draw. Maybe use their shapes to create something completely different.

WARMING UP: DOODLING

Doodling is like daydreaming with a pencil in hand. It's all about letting our imaginations run wild and seeing where our doodles take us. Start by drawing a squiggly line. Now, add some loops, zigzags, and spirals. Let your pencil dance on the paper and see what shapes and creatures emerge from your doodles!

1. Draw a doodle monster! Start with a wiggly line for its body, add big round eyes, and let your imagination go wild with silly features like antennas, squiggly arms, and even some polka dots!

Scribbling is pure fun on paper! Grab your pencil and scribble all over the page. Scribble fast, scribble slow, and watch as lines intertwine and shapes appear. Now, take a step back and see what your scribble looks like. Can you turn it into something amazing? Maybe it's a fierce dragon or a whimsical castle. Let your scribbles guide your imagination!

2. Scribble all over the paper to create a big, wild jungle. Then, turn some scribbles into trees, others into curious animals, and even a few into hidden treasure chests!

Let's challenge our creative brains with shape shuffling! Draw a shape—maybe a circle or a square. Now, transform it into something completely different. That circle could become a smiling face or a bouncing ball. That square could become a towering building or a delicious slice of pizza. The possibilities are endless when we let our shapes take on new forms!

3. **Draw a triangle and transform it into a majestic mountain peak. Add snow, trees, and even a hiker standing on top, enjoying the view!**

Remember, warm-up exercises are all about having fun, letting loose, and exploring your imagination. They're like little adventures that prepare us for the artistic journey ahead. So, grab your pencils, embrace the joy of doodling and scribbling, and get those creative juices flowing!

Now, it's time to unleash your inner artist and embark on a colorful adventure filled with endless possibilities. Are you ready? Let's doodle, scribble, and create masterpieces that will make you say, "Wow, I did that!"

DOODLE PAGE

HOW TO DRAW: FACES

Today, we're going to dive into the exciting world of drawing faces. Faces are like windows to the soul, and by learning to draw them, we can bring characters to life in our artwork. So, grab your pencils and let's explore the wonderful variety of face shapes!

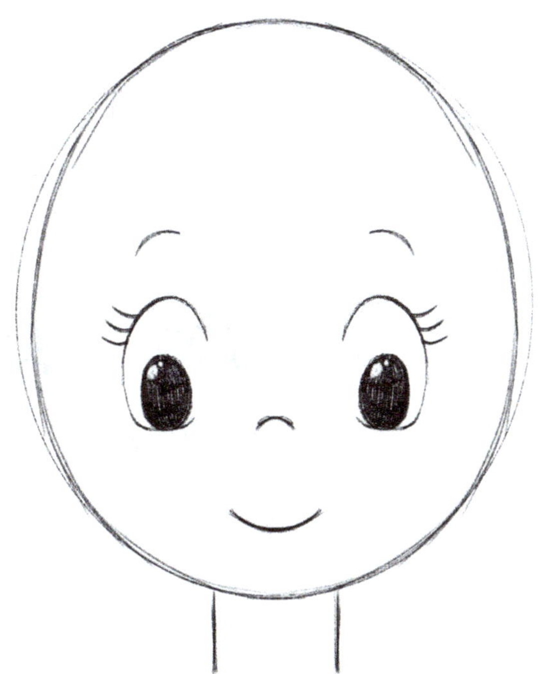

The **round face** shape is as friendly as a sunny day. To draw a round face, start with a big circle. Add two dots for eyes, a curved line for the nose, and a smiling mouth. Don't forget to give your character rosy cheeks to make them extra adorable!

The **square face** shape exudes strength and confidence, that is why angular faces are often used to draw villains. Begin by drawing a square or a rectangle for the face. Place two eyes in the middle, a nose in the lower half, and a thin line for the mouth. Your character will have a strong and determined look!

A **heart-shaped face** is as sweet as a valentine. Draw an upside-down triangle for the face, with the point at the bottom. Add big, sparkling eyes, a small nose, and a sweet smile that mirrors the shape of the face. Your character will melt hearts everywhere!

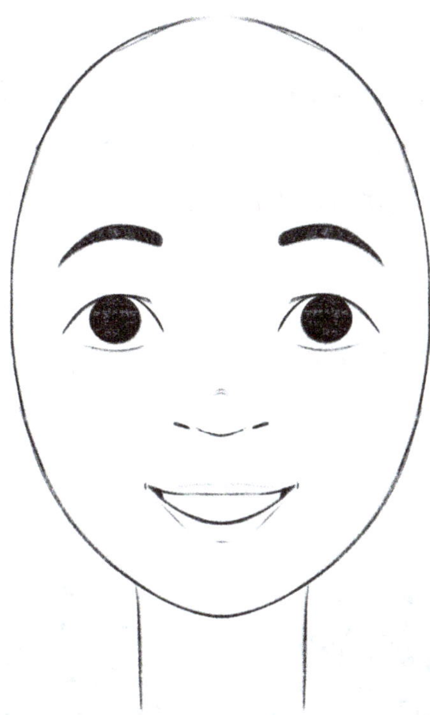

The **oval face shape** is graceful and versatile. Start with an oval shape, slightly longer than it is wide. Place two eyes on the horizontal centerline, a nose below, and a smiling mouth. This face shape is perfect for creating a wide range of characters!

Each face shape tells a unique story. Just like people, characters in our drawings have their own personalities and emotions. By practicing drawing different face shapes, you can create characters with diverse personalities and capture the essence of their emotions. So, let your pencils dance across the paper, experiment with various face shapes, and watch as your characters come to life!

When you experiment with various face shapes, you have the power to breathe life into your characters and capture the essence of their feelings.

Start experimenting with different face shapes and watch as your drawings become filled with a diverse cast of personalities. From the mischievous to the kind-hearted, from the brave to the curious, your characters will express a range of emotions and captivate the hearts of those who see them.

EYES, NOSE AND MOUTH

Faces are like a canvas where emotions come to life, and in this lesson, we'll learn how to draw the key features that make faces so expressive: the eyes, nose, and mouth. So, grab your pencils and let's get started on this fun-filled adventure!

Start by drawing two large circles for the eyes. Add smaller circles inside for the pupils.

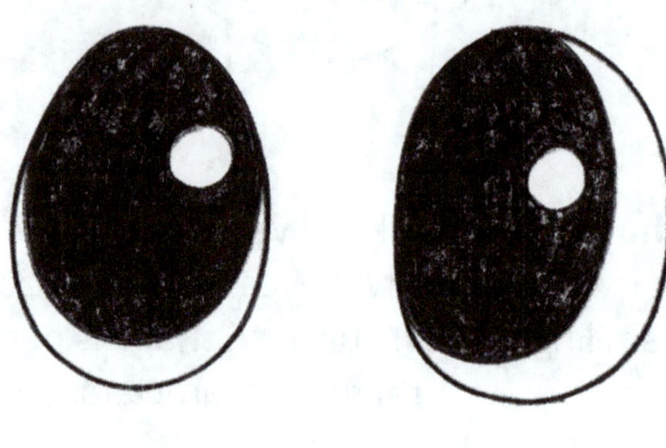

Now, let's make 1

Noses come in all shapes and sizes, and they play a vital role in defining a character's appearance. You can make the nose big, small, pointy, or round —let your creativity soar!

Start with a small curved line for the bridge of the nose. Then, add two small circles for the nostrils.

Experiment with different nose shapes to give your characters their own unique flair.

Draw a cute button nose. Make it small and round, and add some rosy cheeks for extra cuteness!

Draw a big, strawberry-like nose with big nostrils. See the difference?

A smile can brighten up anyone's day, and a frown can express sadness or concern.To create a happy smile, draw an upward curve for the corners of the mouth. For a serious expression, draw a straight line or a gentle downward curve. Let your characters speak through their mouths and express a range of emotions.

Start by drawing a curved line for the top lip and a slightly larger curved line for the bottom lip.

Add emotion to your drawing by trying out different mouths-shapes

Draw a big, wide smile that stretches from ear to ear, showcasing pure joy.

Draw half a smile, with one corner of the mouth turned up in a sinister smirk.

CAPTURING EXPRESSIONS

Faces are like maps of emotions, and observing expressions helps us bring characters to life in our drawings. Look in the mirror or at friends and family. How do their eyes sparkle when they're happy? What happens to their eyebrows when they're surprised? Take mental snapshots of these expressions and try to capture them in your drawings.

DRAW SOME FUNNY FACES ON THESE BLOBS

HOW TO DRAW: STICK FIGURES

Before we dive into drawing dynamic poses, let's understand the significance of stick figures. Stick figures are simple, basic figures made up of straight lines and circles. They serve as the skeleton or framework of our characters, helping us establish proportions and balance. Mastering stick figures is like building a solid foundation for your drawings, enabling you to create more intricate and realistic poses later on. So, let's start with the basics and gradually bring our characters to life!

Begin by drawing **a simple stick figure**. Draw a straight line for the body and a circle for the head. Add two lines for the arms and two lines for the legs. You now have a basic stick figure! Remember, stick figures don't need to be perfect. They're meant to provide a framework for your characters and poses.

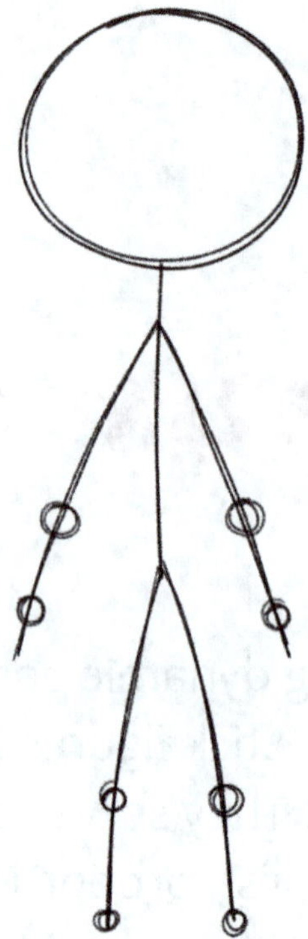

Let's start exploring different poses with a basic standing position. Begin by drawing a stick figure with straight legs and arms hanging down. Add small circles at the joints to represent the joints of the elbows and knees.

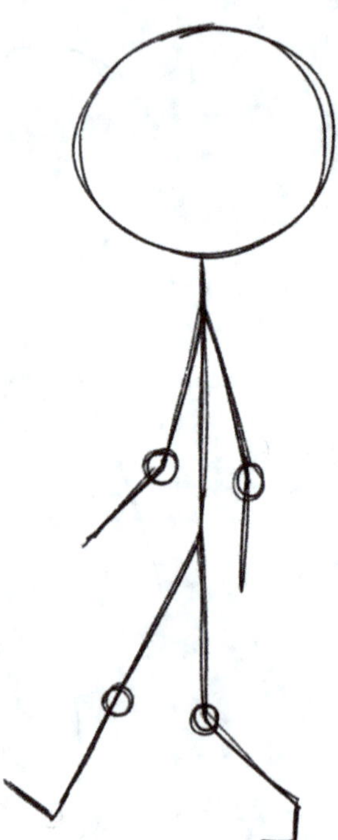

Let's bring some movement to your stick figures with a walking pose. Begin by slightly bending the legs and drawing one leg in front of the other. Add small circles at the joints to represent the bending of the knees and elbows. You can draw lines behind the stick figure to indicate motion.

DRAW STICK FIGURES IN DIFFERENT POSES

DRAW STICK FIGURES IN DIFFERENT POSES

HOW TO DRAW: BUILDING UP STICK FIGURES

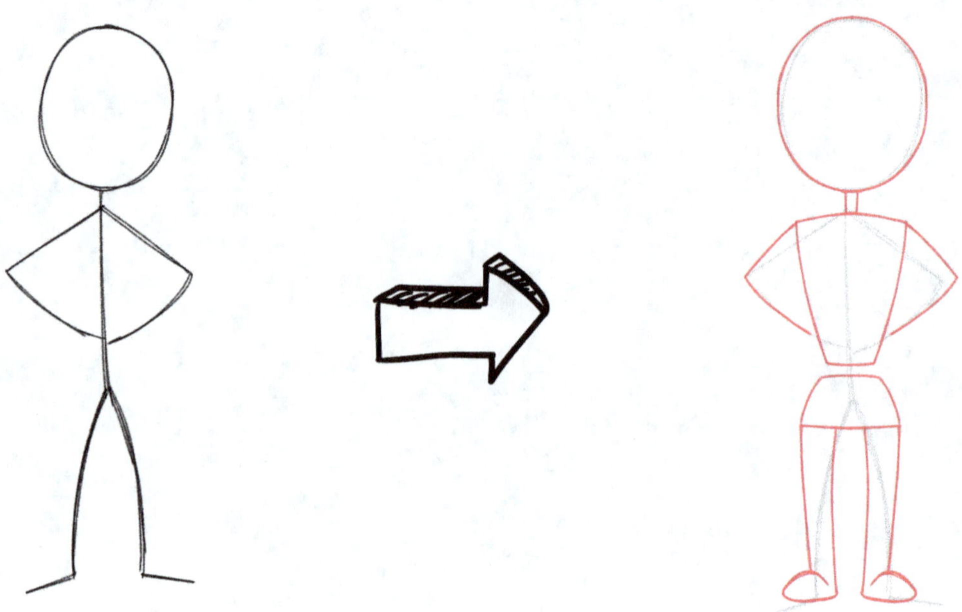

STEP 1

Begin by transforming your stick figure into a more recognizable shape. Start by rounding out the head and body, giving your character a distinct silhouette.

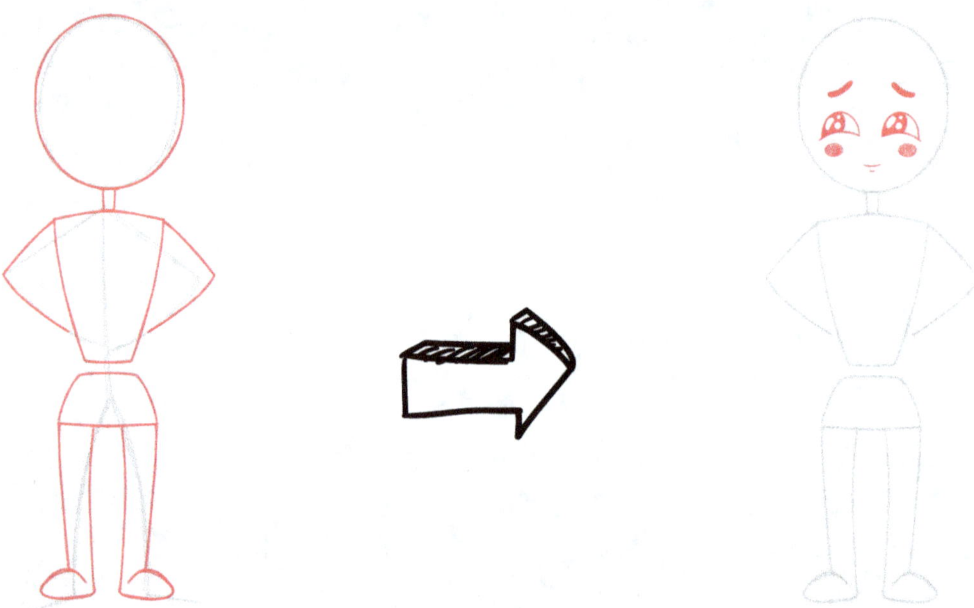

STEP 2

Let's bring emotions to your cartoon characters through expressive faces. Experiment with different eye shapes, eyebrows, and mouth styles to convey different feelings like we practiced before.

HOW TO DRAW: BUILDING UP STICK FIGURES

STEP 3

Dress up your cartoon characters with stylish clothing and accessories. Draw different outfits that match their personality, whether it's a superhero costume, a fancy dress, or casual attire.

STEP 4

Add unique details to make your cartoon characters stand out. Consider adding freckles, scars, or distinctive hairstyles to give them individuality. Play around with different shapes for hands, feet, and body proportions.

HOW TO DRAW: BUILDING UP STICK FIGURES

STEP 4

It's time to infuse your cartoon characters with vibrant colors. Use your imagination to choose colors that represent their personalities.

YOUR TURN!

Remember, the journey from a simple stick figure to a lively cartoon character is all about embracing your creativity and having fun. Practice, experiment, and let your imagination soar. With each drawing, you'll discover new techniques and develop your unique

HOW TO DRAW: PERSPECTIVE

Perspective helps create the illusion of depth, making your art come to life. So, get ready to have fun and learn some easy techniques to add depth to your drawings! In this chapter, we will explore how to make your drawings look three-dimensional and realistic by understanding the concepts of the horizon line and vanishing point.

When we talk about perspective, we mean creating the feeling of **distance and space** in a drawing. It's like looking at something in real life and trying to capture its depth on a flat piece of paper. Let's start with two important concepts: the horizon line and vanishing point.

The horizon line is like the line where the sky meets the ground when you look into the distance. To draw it, simply make a straight line across your paper. This line will help you determine where objects should be placed and how far they are from you.

Now, imagine a special point on the horizon line called **the vanishing point**. It's like a spot where everything seems to disappear into the distance. You can mark it with a dot or a small X. The vanishing point helps you create depth and perspective in your drawings.

One easy technique to create depth is called one-point perspective. Start by drawing a simple shape, like a square or rectangle, on your paper. Imagine that all the lines of the shape are parallel to each other and extend towards the vanishing point. Connect the corners of the shape to the vanishing point with straight lines. This makes the shape look like it's going back into the distance.

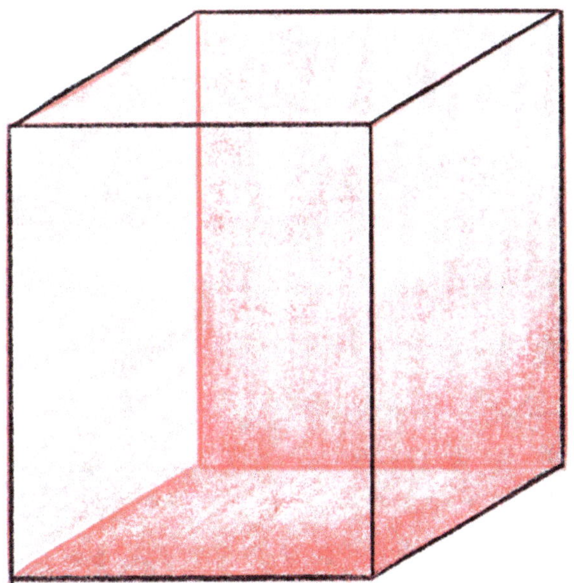

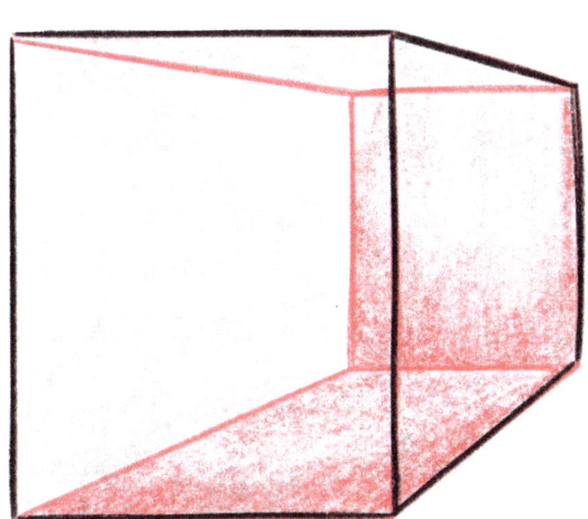

As you practice perspective, remember that objects appear smaller as they move away from you. So, when drawing things in the distance, make them smaller and use lighter, less detailed lines. This will give your drawings a sense of depth.

Another way to add depth is by overlapping objects. Imagine you're looking at a row of trees. Some trees will appear in front of others, partially covering them. By drawing objects in a way that they overlap, you give the impression that they are at different distances from you. This technique is like adding layers to your drawing and can make it more interesting to look at.

Shadows are like magical companions that bring your drawings to life. They help define the form of objects and show how they interact with light. When adding shadows, think about the direction of light in your drawing. Imagine where the light is coming from and how it would cast shadows. Shadows should be drawn under objects and on the ground, following the direction of the light source. By incorporating shadows, you'll add depth and dimension to your drawings.

Select a scene or subject for your drawing. It could be a landscape, a room, a still life arrangement, or anything that sparks your imagination. Make sure your chosen scene has a variety of objects and elements that will allow you to practice creating depth and adding shadows.

HOW TO DRAW: COLORS

Get ready to unleash your creativity and learn
how to use colors to make your artwork come alive!
Colors are like magic potions that can evoke different emotions and
moods. Understanding how colors work together can help you create
stunning and harmonious artworks. So, let's embark on this colorful
adventure!

PRIMARY COLORS

Our best buddies on this artistic journey are pencils. They come in
different sizes and hardness. Just like Goldilocks, we need to find the
one that's "just right" for us. Try different pencils and see which one
feels comfy in your hand. Remember, pencils love to dance on paper,
so hold them gently and let them glide!

SECONDARY COLORS

When you mix two primary colors together, you create secondary colors. Mixing red and blue gives you purple, mixing red and yellow creates orange, and mixing blue and yellow produces green. Secondary colors are vibrant and full of life!

When you mix a **primary color** with a **secondary color** you get a **tertiary color.**

WARM AND COOL COLORS

Colors can be divided into warm and cool categories. Warm colors, such as red, orange, and yellow, remind us of warmth and energy. Cool colors, like blue, green, and purple, evoke a sense of calmness and tranquility.

COLOR WHEEL

The color wheel is a magical tool that helps us understand how colors relate to each other. It's like a rainbow circle with all the colors arranged in a specific order. The primary colors are at the center, followed by the secondary and tertiary colors. Exploring the color wheel can guide you in choosing complementary (opposite) colors or analogous (next to each other) colors for your artwork.

Remember, the most important thing is to have fun and let your imagination guide you. Experiment with colors, try new combinations, and don't be afraid to make mistakes. Each color you use brings a new dimension to your artwork and reflects your unique style and creativity.

So, grab your paintbrushes, colored pencils, or markers, and let the colors dance across your canvas! Immerse yourself in the fascinating world of color and watch as your artwork bursts with life and brilliance.

TIPS FOR COLORING

Coloring is a fantastic way to express your creativity and bring your artwork to life. Here are some fun tips and tricks to take your coloring skills to the next level:

START WITH A LIGHT TOUCH

When coloring, begin with a light touch. This way, you can gradually build up the color intensity and create smooth and even shades. Remember, you can always add more color, but it's harder to remove it once it's too dark.

STAY WITHIN THE LINES (OR NOT!)

Coloring inside the lines can help your artwork look neat and tidy, but it's also okay to break the rules and let your imagination run wild. Feel free to experiment and color outside the lines if it suits your artistic vision. It's all about expressing yourself!

MIX AND MATCH

Don't be afraid to mix colors together! Explore blending different colors to create new shades and gradients. Start by coloring two colors next to each other and then gently blend them together using small circular motions. It's like creating your own magical color potions!

PLAY WITH TEXTURES

Coloring doesn't always have to be smooth. You can add texture and depth to your artwork by using different techniques. Try using small dots, hatching (drawing parallel lines), or even cross-hatching (drawing intersecting lines) to give your coloring a unique and interesting look.

HIGHLIGHT AND SHINE

To make your artwork pop, add highlights! Leave some areas uncolored or use a white crayon or colored pencil to create highlights and shiny spots. This technique adds dimension and makes your artwork more eye-catching.

EXPERIMENT WITH COLOR SCHEMES

Don't limit yourself to realistic colors. Play around with different color schemes to create exciting and unexpected combinations. Use your imagination to color a blue sun or a purple tree. Let your creativity soar!

USE DIFFERENT MATERIALS

Don't restrict yourself to just one coloring tool. Try different materials like colored pencils, markers, or watercolor paints. Each medium has its unique qualities, and experimenting with them will give your artwork a fresh and diverse look.

Coloring should be a fun and relaxing activity. Remember to take breaks, stretch your hand, and enjoy the process. You can listen to your favorite music, chat with friends, or even color together with family members. Let the joy of coloring fill your heart!

After finishing your coloring masterpiece, you can take it a step further by personalizing it. Add your name, a date, or even some fun stickers around the edges. It's a wonderful way to make your artwork uniquely yours.

Finally, don't forget to proudly share your artwork with others. Display it on the fridge, create a gallery on your wall, or even gift it to someone special. Your artwork is a reflection of your creativity, and it deserves to be celebrated!

HOW TO DRAW: ANIMALS

It's time to dive into the fascinating world of domestic animals. These furry friends bring joy and companionship to our lives, and we're going to learn how to draw them step-by-step. Get your pencils ready, and let's embark on an artistic adventure with some adorable domestic animals!

INDEX

HOW TO DRAW: A DOG

Let's start with our faithful companions, dogs! Draw a big circle for the head, add two floppy ears on top, and a curved line for the body. Then, add legs, a wagging tail, and a friendly face. Woof!

YOUR TURN!

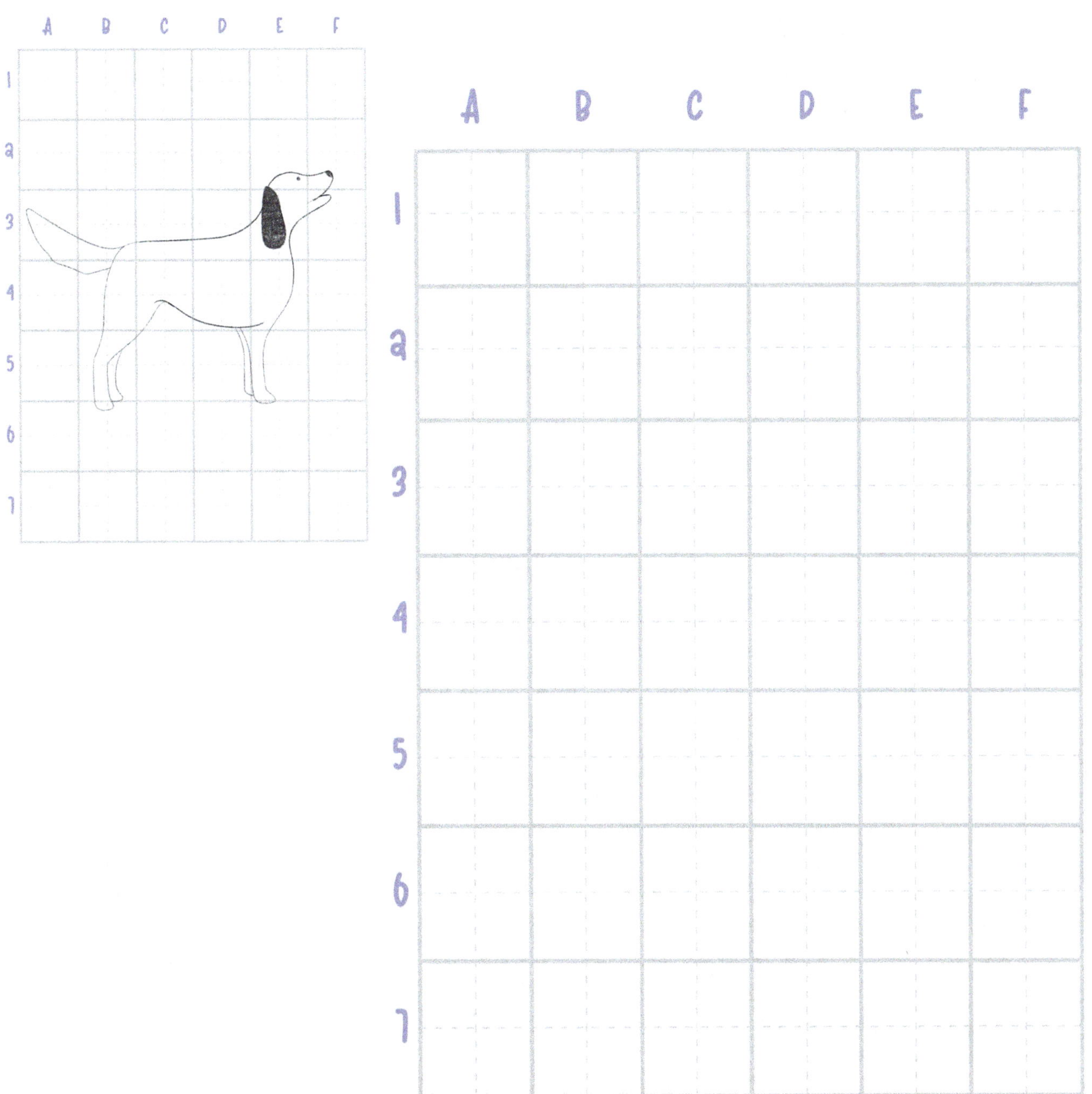

Fun Fact

Did you know that dogs have an incredible sense of smell? They can sniff out all sorts of things, like missing socks and even hidden treats!

HOW TO DRAW: A CAT

Cats are graceful and mysterious. Begin with an oval shape for the head, then add pointy ears and a small triangular nose. Draw a curvy body, four legs, and a long tail. Meow!

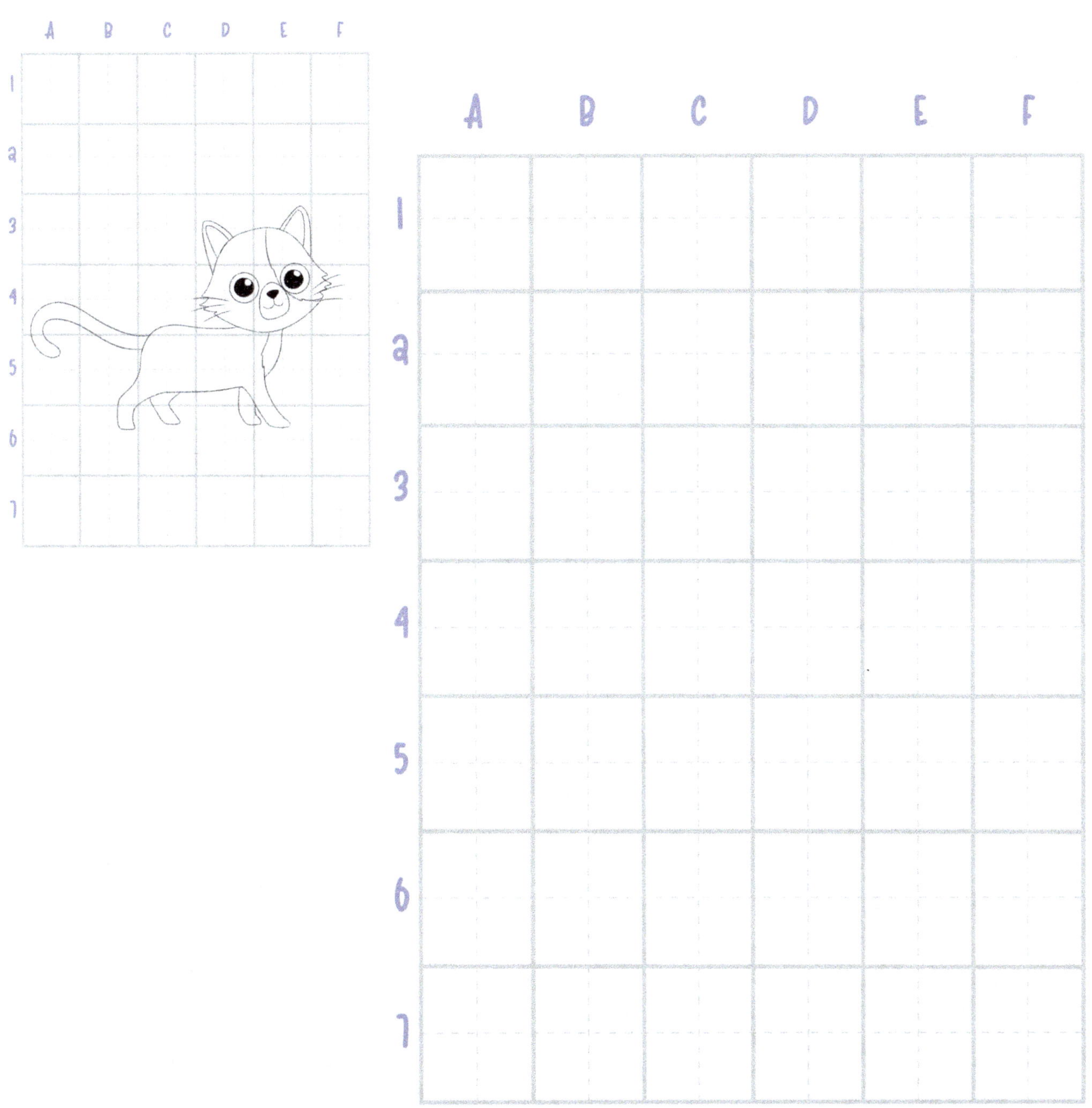

Joke
Why don't cats play board games in the wild?

Answer: Too many cheetahs!

HOW TO DRAW: A RABBIT

Hop into drawing a cute bunny! Start with a big circle for the head, and add long ears on top. Draw a rounded body and paws. Don't forget the fluffy tail! Hippity-hop!

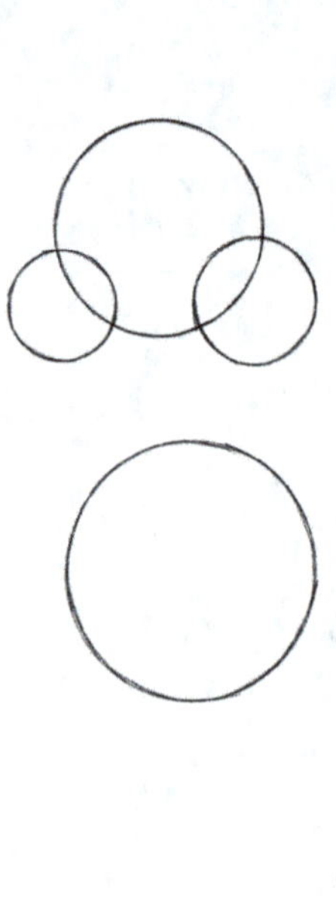 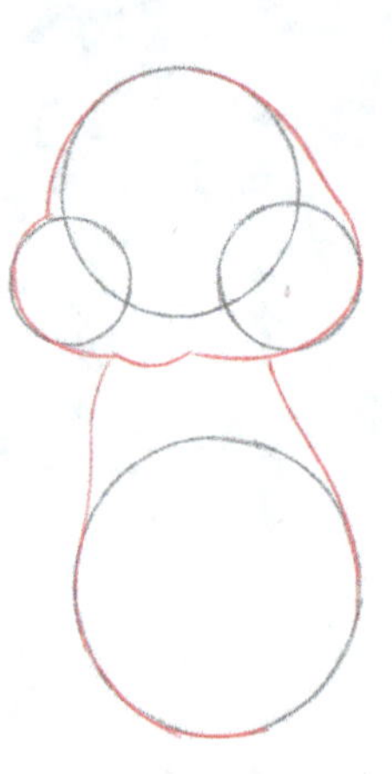 

YOUR TURN!

HOW TO DRAW: A BIRD

Let's soar into drawing a bird! Begin with a small circle for the head. Add a pointy beak and two round eyes. Draw a triangular body and wings. Don't forget to include colorful feathers! Tweet-tweet!

YOUR TURN!

Joke

What do you call a bird that's afraid of heights?

Answer: A chicken!

HOW TO DRAW: A FISH

Dive into the underwater world by drawing a fish! Start with an oval shape for the body. Add a triangle for the tail and fins. Don't forget to give your fishy some big, round eyes. Glub-glub!

YOUR TURN!

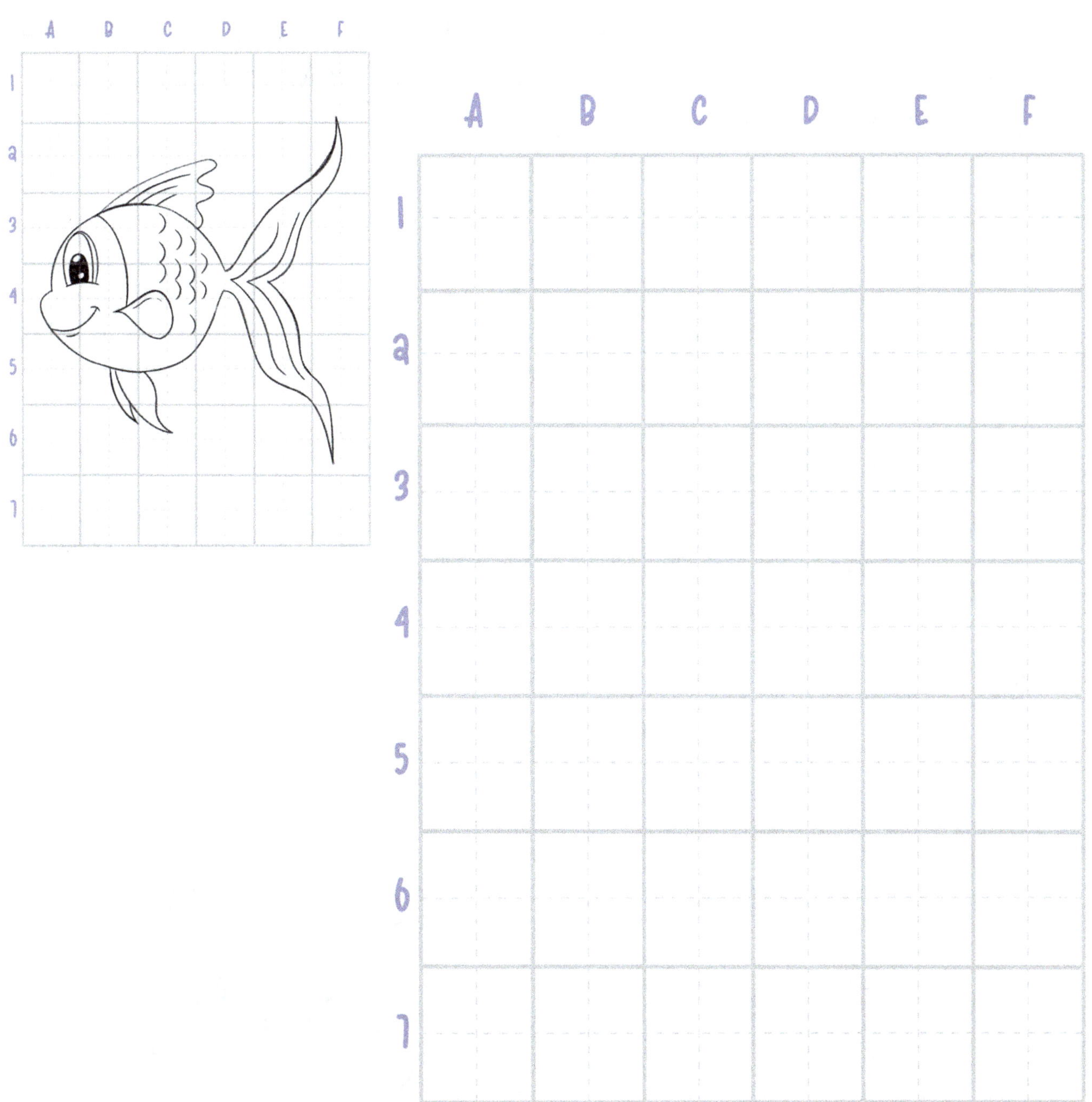

Fun Fact

Fish live in all kinds of habitats, from freshwater lakes to salty oceans. They are excellent swimmers and have gills that help them breathe underwater.

HOW TO DRAW: A HAMSTER

Get ready to draw a tiny, adorable hamster! Begin with a small oval for the body. Add small, round ears and a cute, tiny nose. Draw little paws and a fluffy tail. Squeak-squeak!

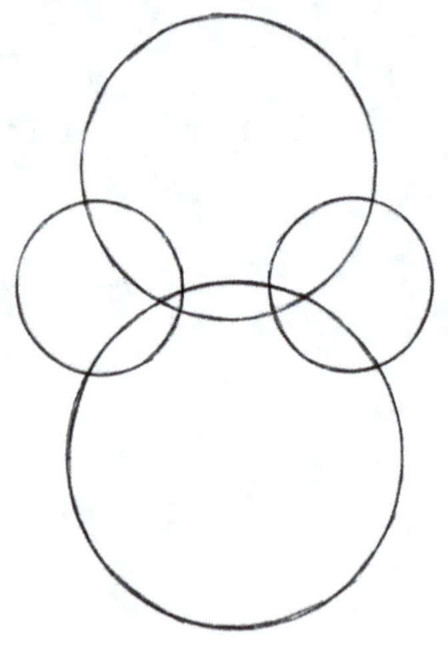 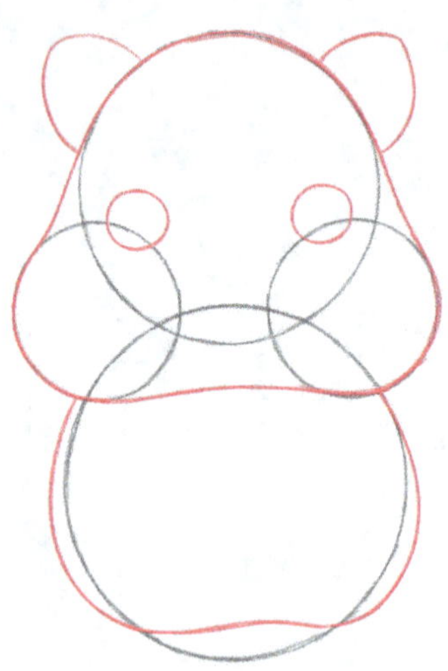 

YOUR TURN!

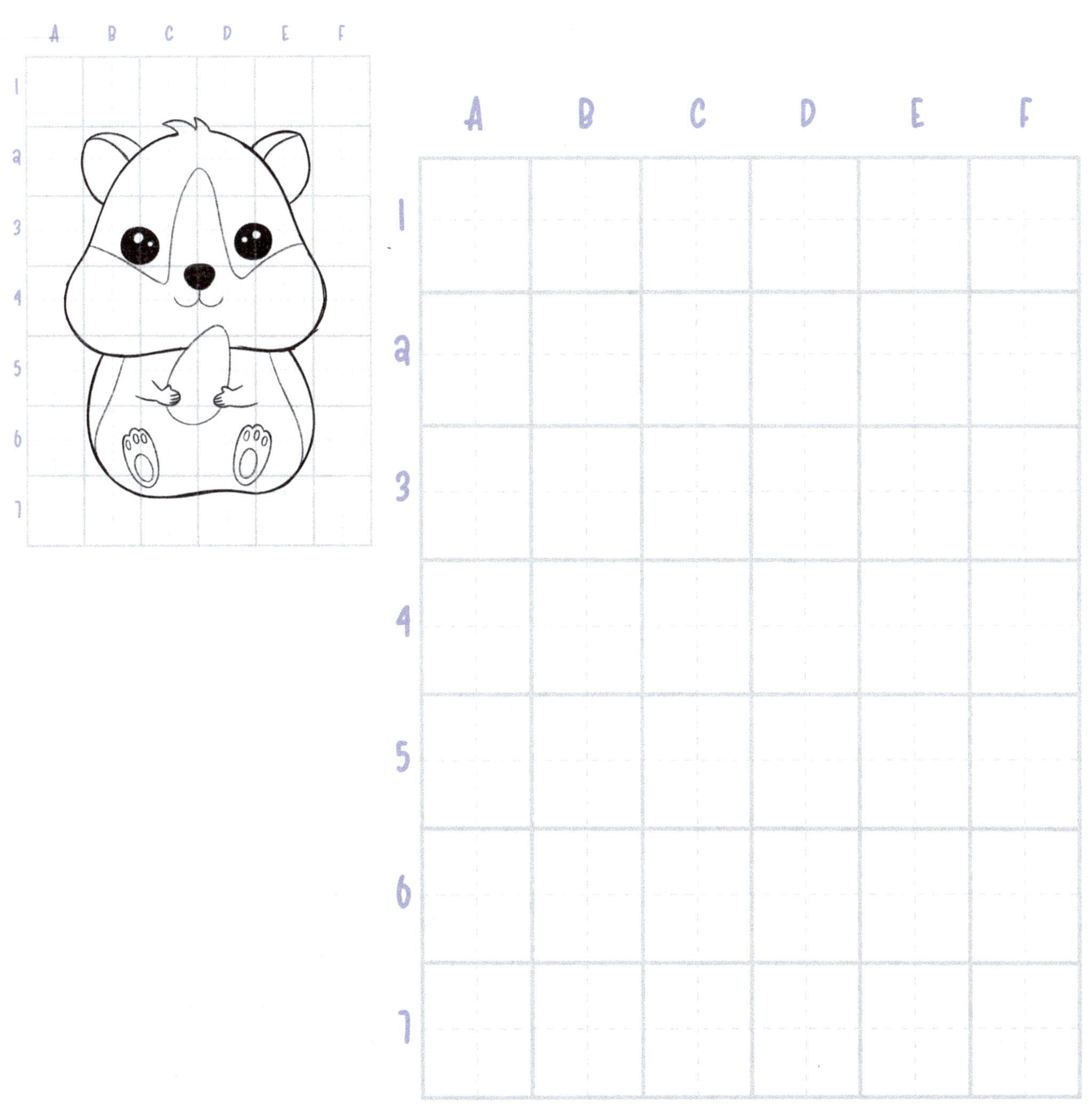

Joke

What do you call a hamster that isn't a professional?

Answer: A hamateur!

HOW TO DRAW: A TURTLE

Let's slow down and draw a turtle! Start with a big oval for the shell. Add a small head sticking out and four short legs. Don't forget to draw the pattern on the shell. Slow and steady wins the race!

YOUR TURN!

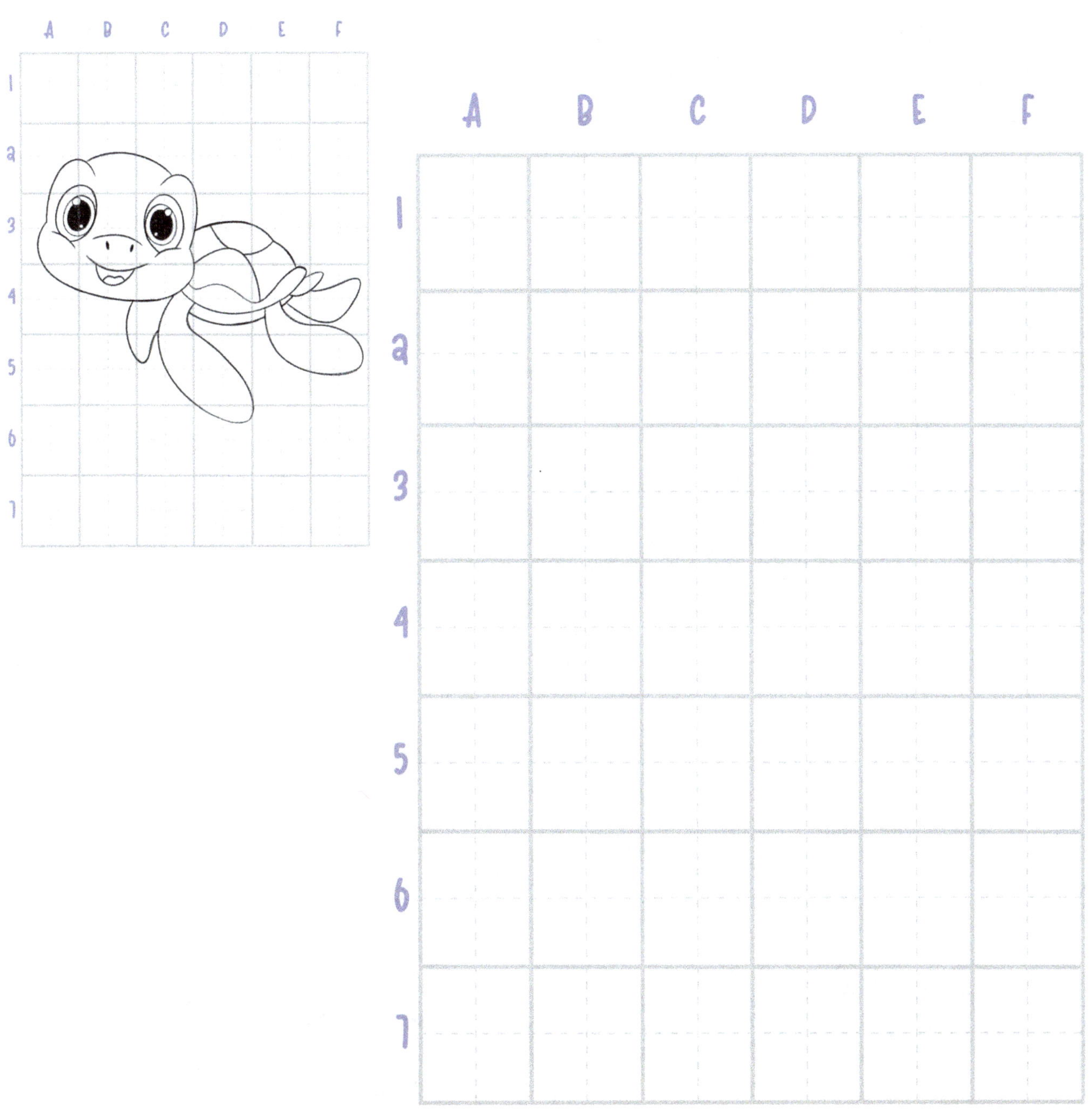

HOW TO DRAW: A GUINEA PIG

Time to draw a fluffy guinea pig! Begin with a rounded body. Add small, round ears and a little face with a tiny nose. Draw short legs and give your guinea pig some whiskers. Wheek-wheek!

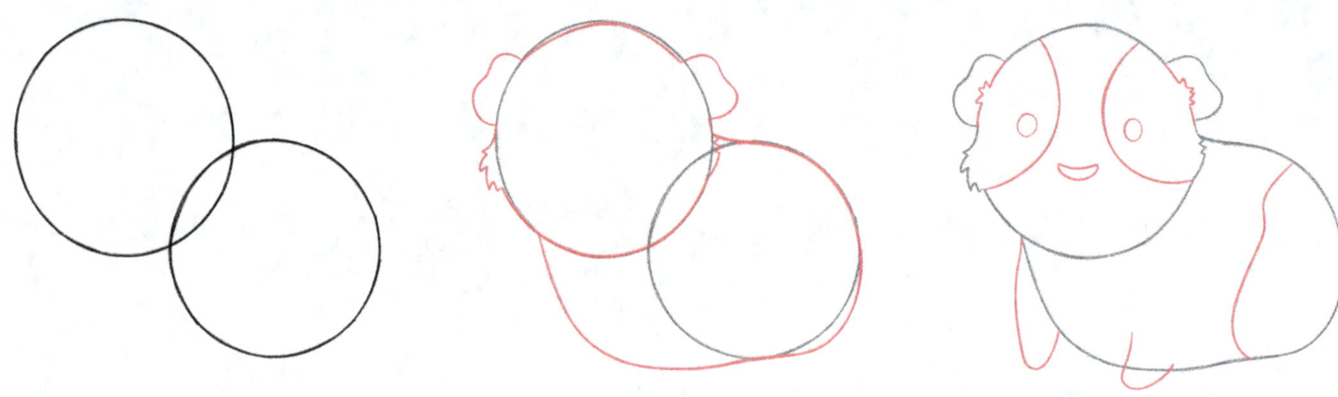

YOUR TURN!

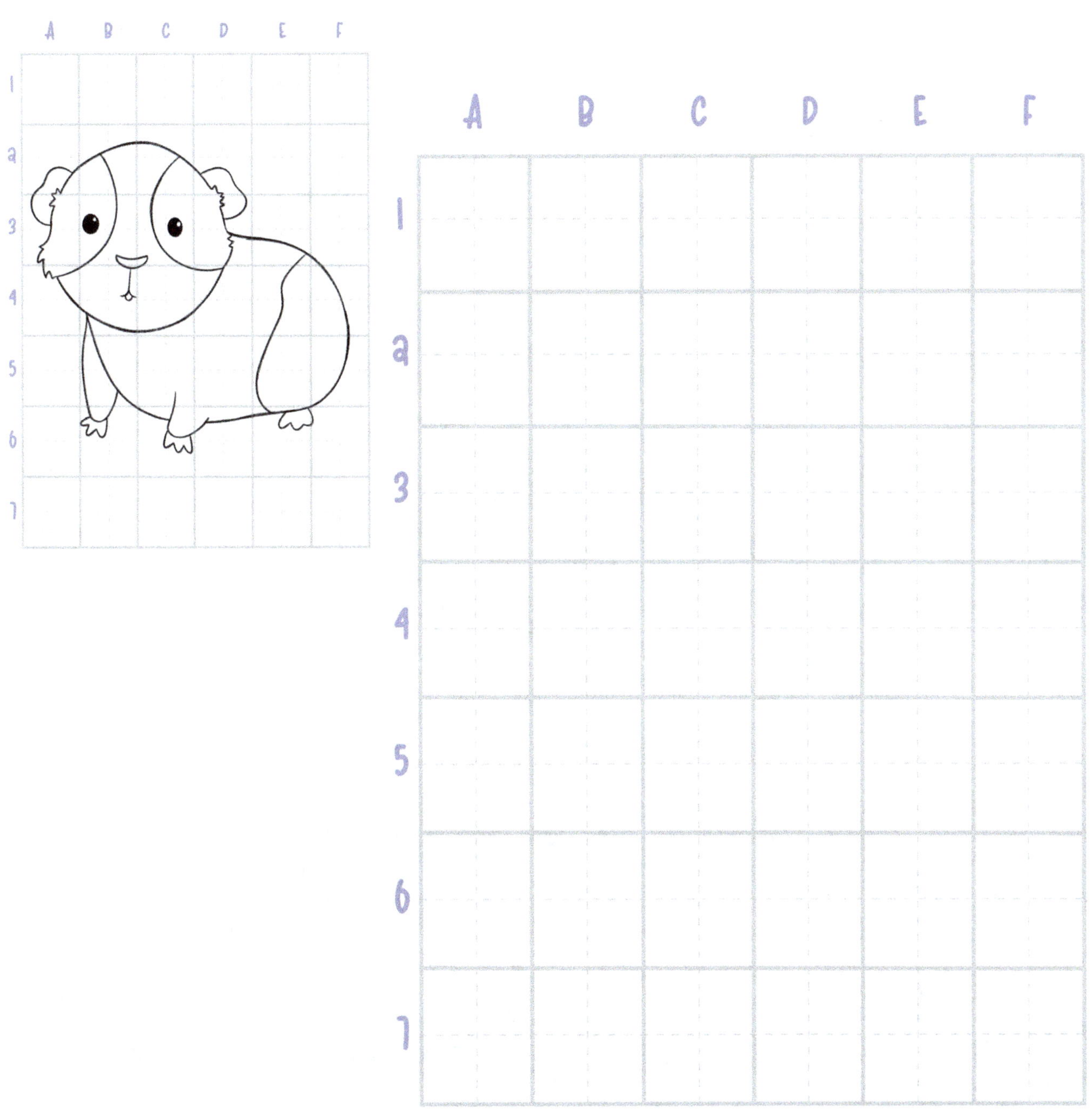

Joke
What is a Guinea pig's favorite unit of time?

Answer: Wheeks!

HOW TO DRAW: A HORSE

Let's gallop into drawing a majestic horse! Start with a big oval for the body. Add a long neck, a head with pointy ears, and a flowing mane. Draw four legs and a swishy tail. Giddy up!

YOUR TURN!

<u>Fun Fact</u>

Horses can run really fast. In fact, some horses can gallop at speeds of up to 40 miles per hour! That's as fast as a car on the highway!

HOW TO DRAW: A CHICKEN

Let's gallop into drawing a majestic horse! Start with a big oval for the body. Add a long neck, a head with pointy ears, and a flowing mane. Draw four legs and a swishy tail. Giddy up!

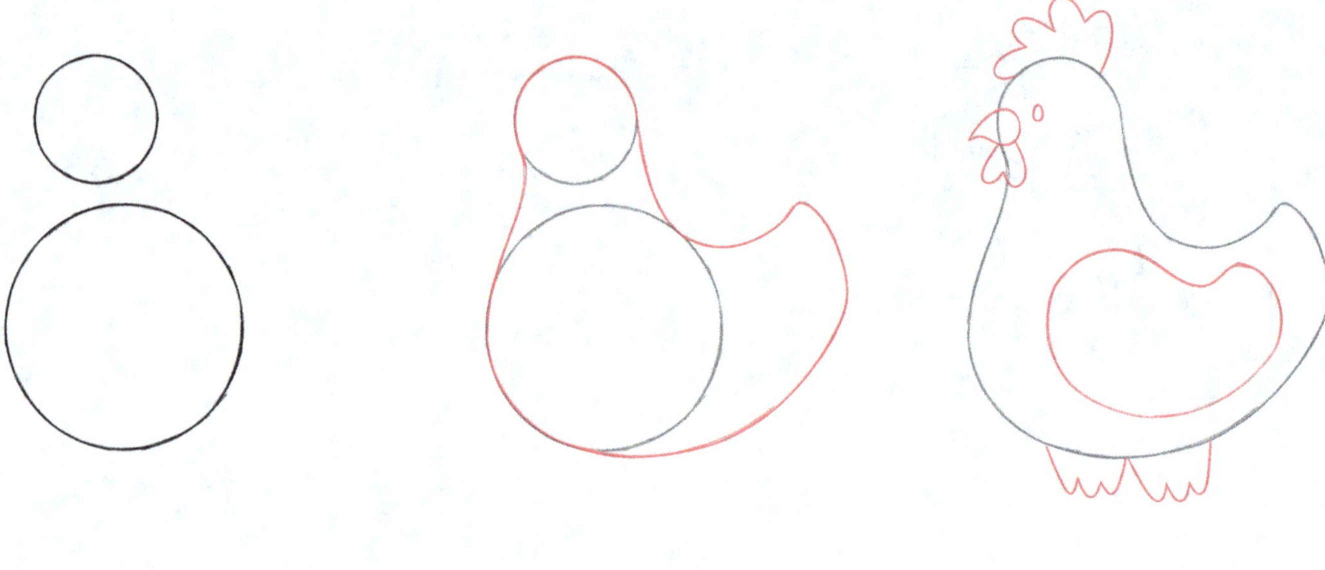

YOUR TURN!

A B C D E F
A B C D E F
1
2
3
4
5
6
7

Joke
How do chickens wake up on time?

Answer: Alarm clucks!

HOW TO DRAW: A LION

Begin with a large circle for the head. Add a big, flowing mane around the face. Draw a long body, four strong legs, and a tail with a fluffy tip. Roar like a lion!

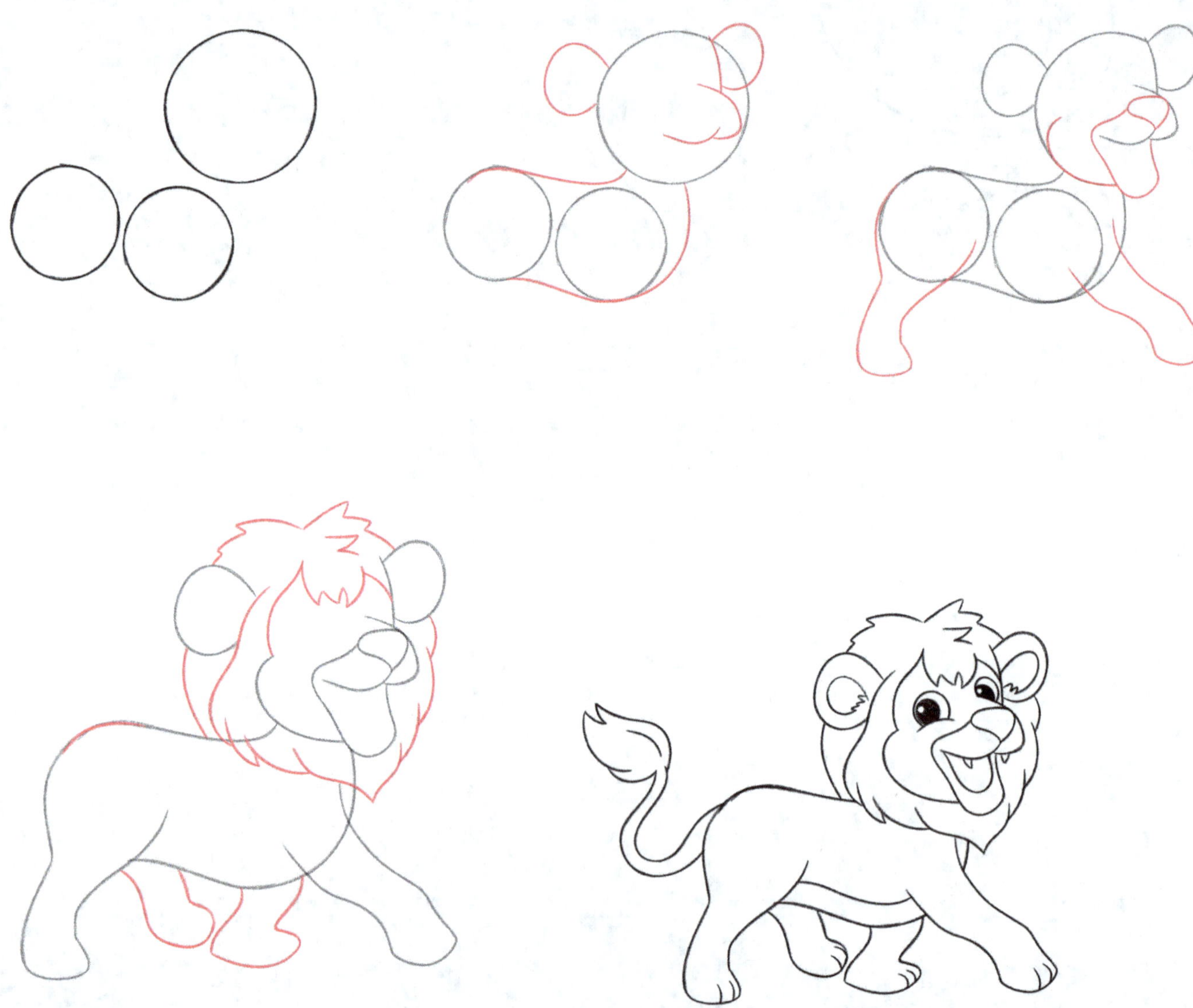

YOUR TURN!

Fun Fact

Lions eat a LOT! In a single meal, lions can eat up to 40 kg of meat, or almost a fourth of their body weight.

HOW TO DRAW: AN ELEPHANT

Start with a big oval shape for the body. Add a large head and two long, curvy tusks. Draw four sturdy legs and a tail. Don't forget to add those floppy ears! Trumpet like an elephant!

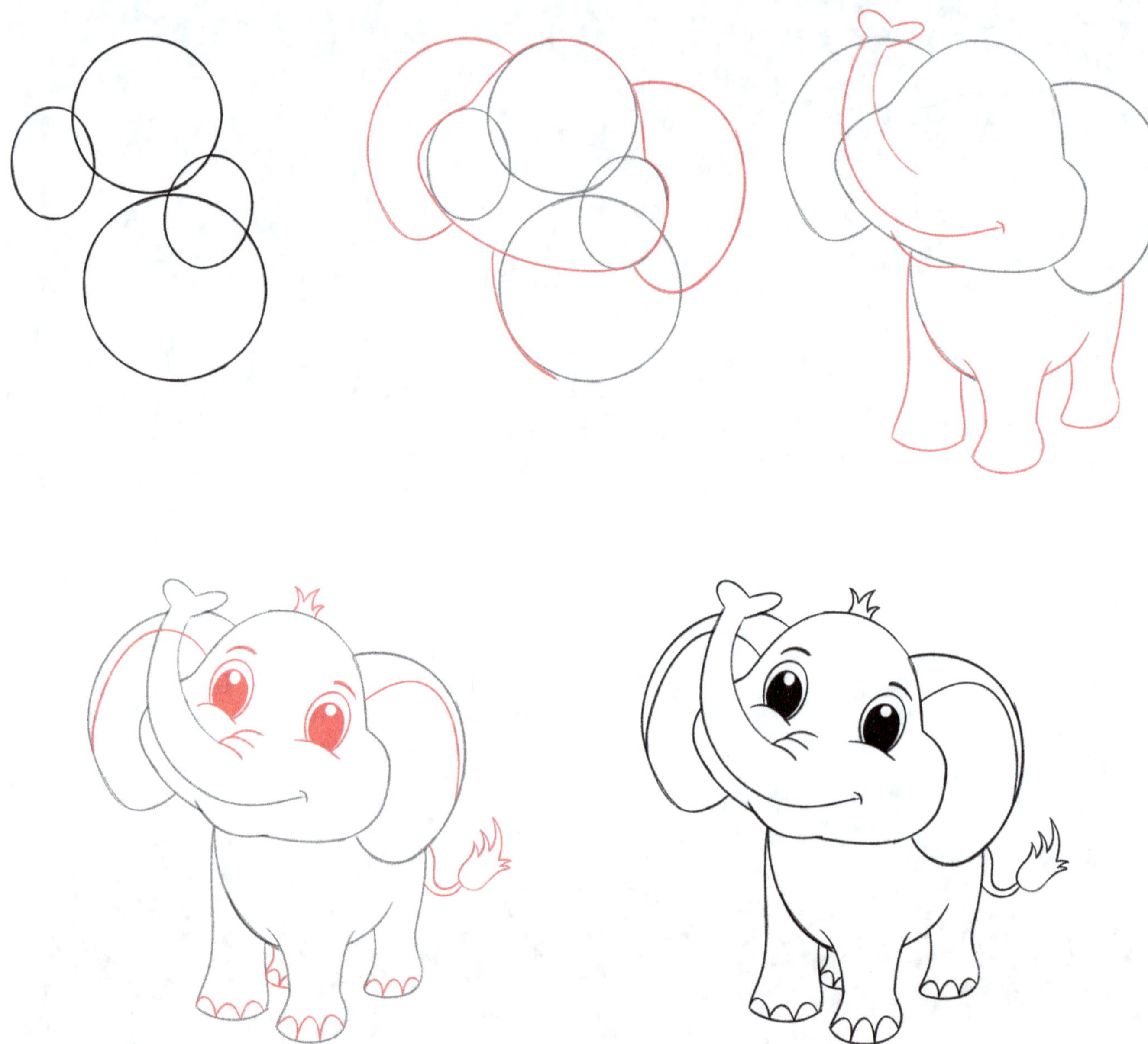

YOUR TURN!

Joke

What do you get when you cross an elephant with a fish?

Answer: Swimming trunks!

HOW TO DRAW: A GIRAFFE

Let's reach new heights and draw a giraffe! Begin with a long, thin rectangle for the body. Add a long neck with a small oval head on top. Draw four long legs and those signature spots. Stretch like a giraffe!

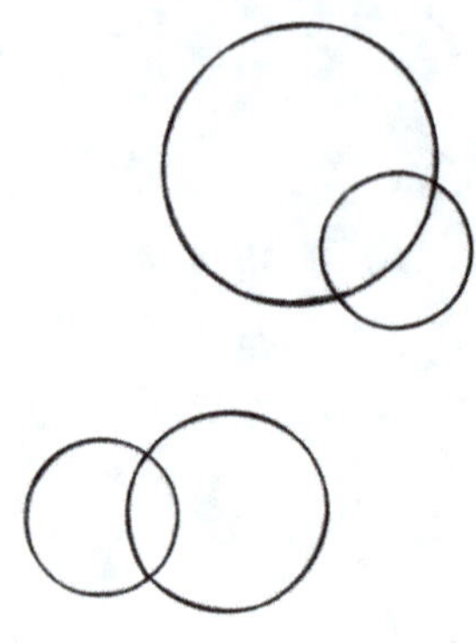 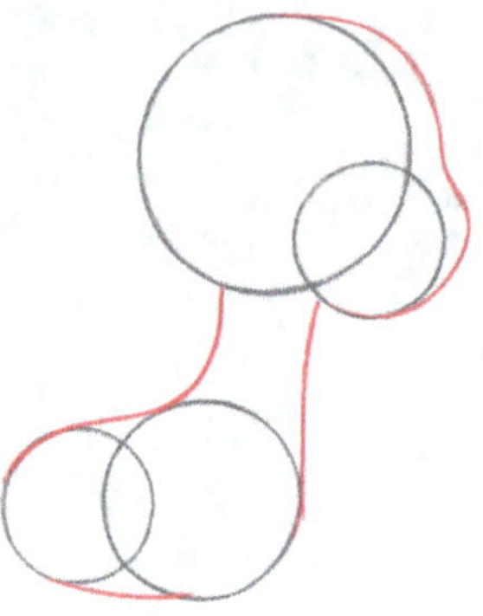 

YOUR TURN!

Fun Fact

The tallest mammals on Earth are giraffes. They stand around 6 feet taller than most people only on their legs!

HOW TO DRAW: A TIGER

Start with a big circle for the head. Add pointy ears and draw bold stripes across the face and body. Draw a long body, four strong legs, and a tail with stripes. Growl like a tiger!

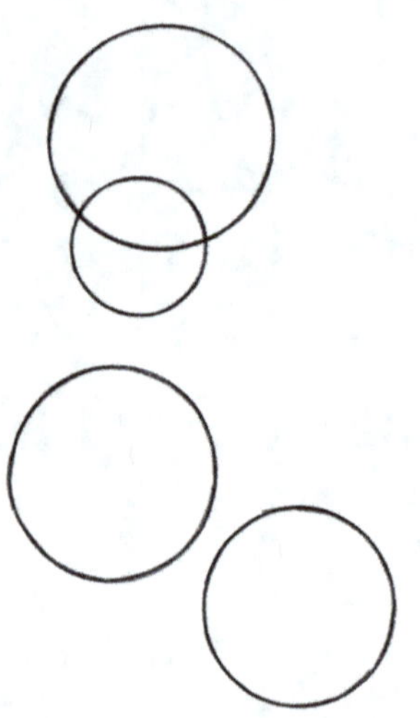 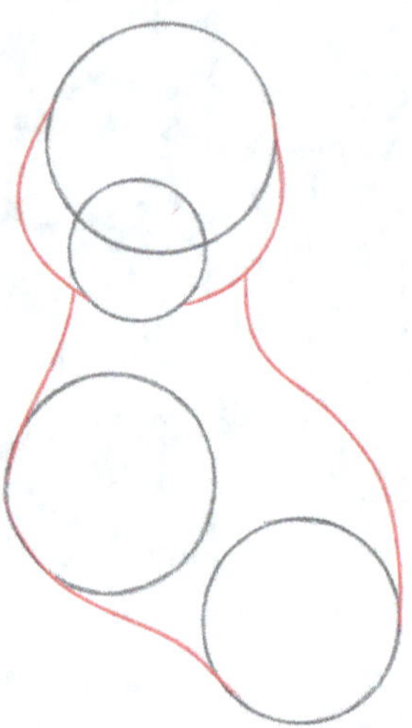 

YOUR TURN!

Joke

How do tigers describe themselves?

Answer: Purr-fect!

HOW TO DRAW: A MONKEY

Let's swing into drawing a playful monkey! Begin with a small circle for the head. Add two round ears and a big smile. Draw a curvy body, arms with hands, and a long tail. Jump around like a monkey!

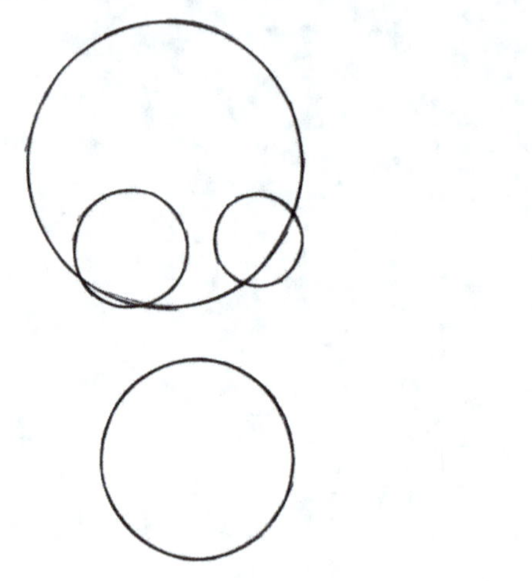 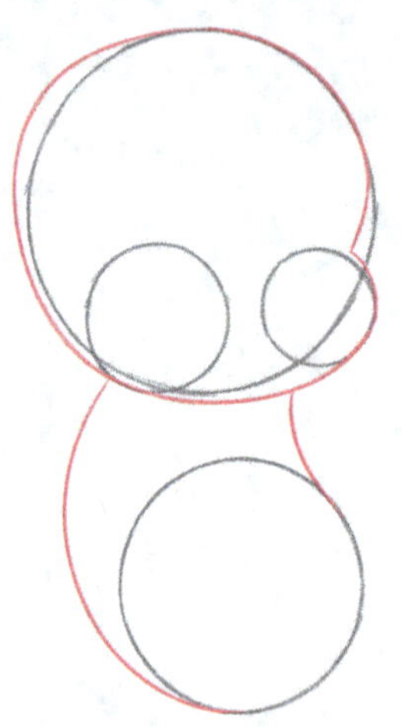 

YOUR TURN!

HOW TO DRAW: A PANDA

Start with a big oval for the body. Add a round head with two cute, black ears. Draw black patches around the eyes. Give your panda big paws and a fluffy tail. Eat bamboo like a panda!

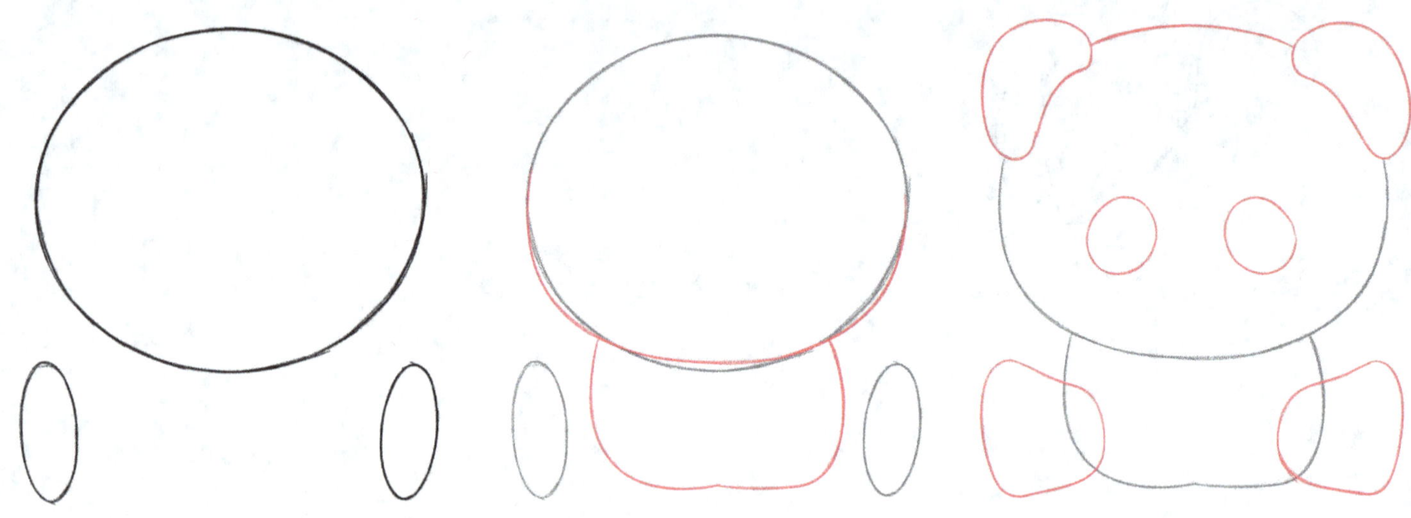

YOUR TURN!

HOW TO DRAW: A ZEBRA

Let's gallop into drawing a zebra! Begin with a large rectangle for the body. Add a small, round head and pointy ears. Draw bold stripes all over the body and legs. Trot like a zebra!

Fun Fact

Zebras distinguishing black and white stripes are as recognizable as a person's fingerprint. When a foal is born, its stripes are reddish-brown, but as it grows, they turn black.

HOW TO DRAW: A KANGAROO

Start with a large oval shape for the body. Add a small head with two pointy ears. Draw powerful hind legs for hopping and smaller front legs. Don't forget that long, strong tail. Bounce like a kangaroo!

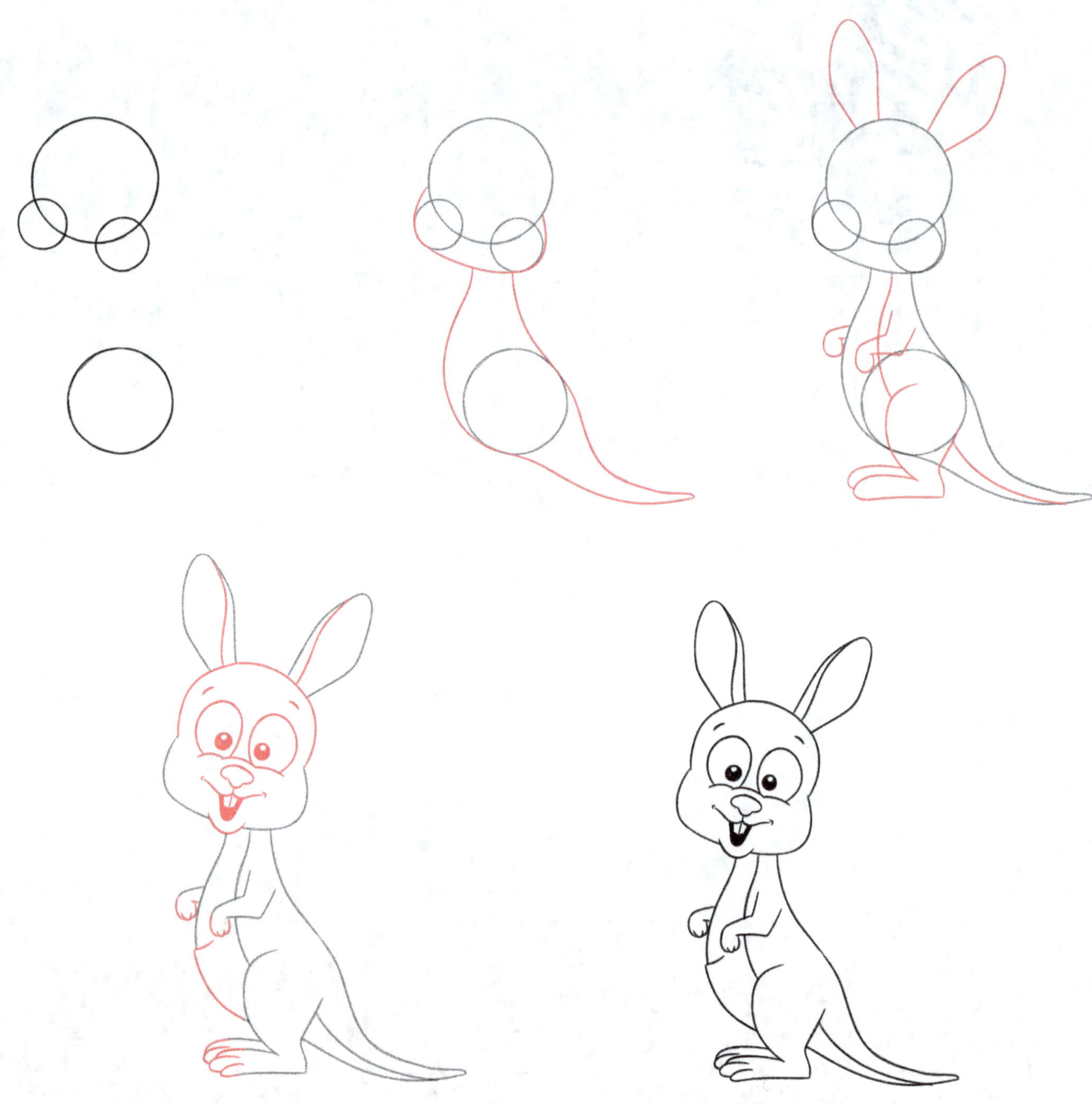

YOUR TURN!

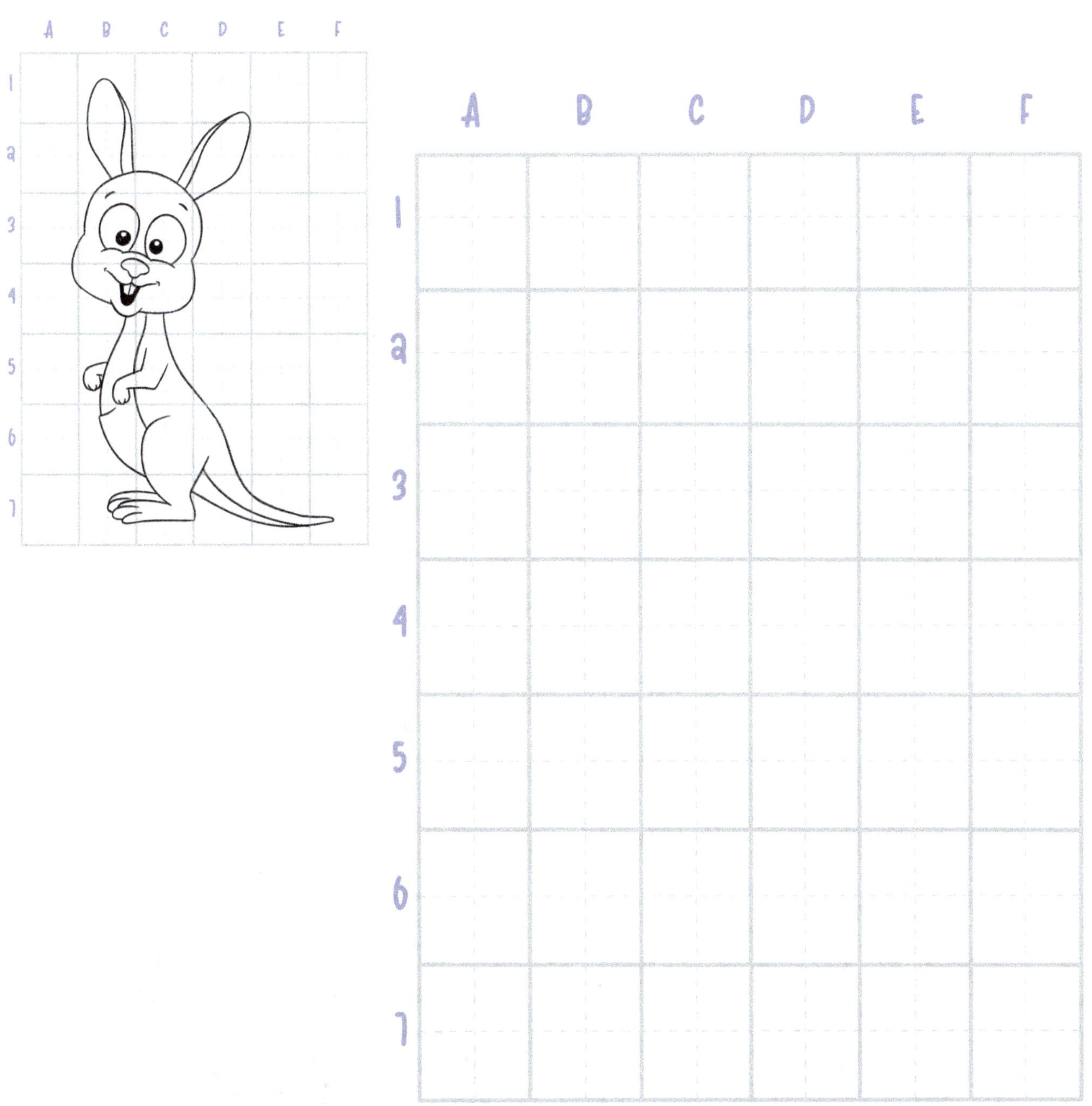

Joke
What do you call a lazy baby kangaroo?

Answer: A pouch potato!

HOW TO DRAW: A CHEETAH

Let's race into drawing a speedy cheetah! Begin with a long, curvy body. Add a small head and pointy ears. Draw spots all over the body. Make sure to include those long legs built for speed. Sprint like a cheetah!

YOUR TURN!

Fun Fact

Cheetahs are the world's fastest land animals over short distances, capable of reaching speeds of up to 64 miles per hour in under three seconds.

HOW TO DRAW: A CROCODILE

Start with a long, curved shape for the body. Add a wide, V-shaped mouth with sharp teeth. Draw short, stubby legs and a long tail. Watch out for that powerful bite! Snap like a crocodile!

YOUR TURN!

<u>Joke</u>
What's the difference between a dog and a crocodile?

Answer: The dog's bark is worst than his bite!

HOW TO DRAW: MYSTICAL CREATURES

It's time to dive into the fascinating world of domestic animals. These furry friends bring joy and companionship to our lives, and we're going to learn how to draw them step-by-step. Get your pencils ready, and let's embark on an artistic adventure with some adorable domestic animals!

INDEX

HOW TO DRAW: A UNICORN

Start with a large circle for the head. Add a long, graceful curved line for the body. Draw four slender legs and a flowing mane. Don't forget the most magical part – a long, spiraling horn on the forehead. Sparkle like a unicorn!

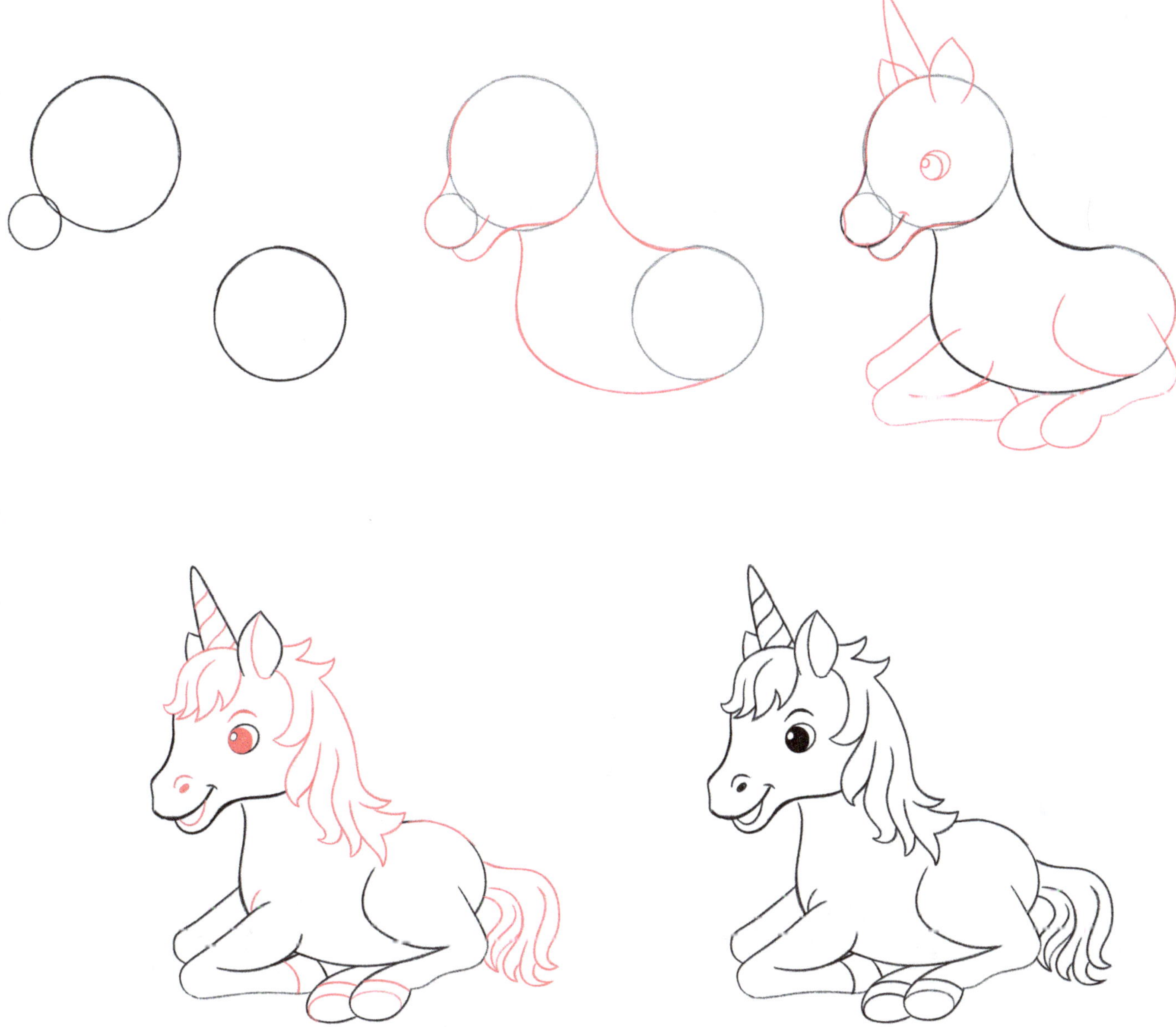

YOUR TURN!

<u>Fun Fact</u>

Cheetahs are the world's fastest land animals over short distances, capable of reaching speeds of up to 64 miles per hour in under three seconds.

HOW TO DRAW: A DRAGON

Begin with a big oval for the body. Add a long, snaky neck and a triangular head. Draw wings on the back and sharp claws on the feet. Don't forget to give your dragon a fiery breath. Roar like a dragon!

YOUR TURN!

<u>Joke</u>

What's the difference between a dog and a crocodile?

Answer: The dog's bark is worst than his bite!

HOW TO DRAW: A MERMAID

Let's dive into drawing a mystical mermaid or merman! Begin with a curvy line for the body. Add a fish tail at the bottom and a human-like torso at the top. Draw flowing hair and a friendly face. Swim like a mermaid/merman!

YOUR TURN!

Fun Fact
Cheetahs are the world's fastest land animals over short distances, capable of reaching speeds of up to 64 miles per hour in under three seconds.

HOW TO DRAW: A FAIRY

Start with a small circle for the head. Add delicate wings on the back. Draw a curvy body and arms with dainty hands. Don't forget to give your fairy a mischievous smile. Sprinkle some fairy dust and fly like a fairy!

YOUR TURN!

Joke

What's the difference between a dog and a crocodile?

Answer: The dog's bark is worst than his bite!

HOW TO DRAW: A GNOME

Start with a round head. Add a small, stout body with chubby arms and legs. Draw a pointy hat on top of the head and a long, white beard. Give your gnome a mischievous smile and a pair of rosy cheeks. Let the magic of the garden inspire your gnome drawing!

YOUR TURN!

Fun Fact

Cheetahs are the world's fastest land animals over short distances, capable of reaching speeds of up to 64 miles per hour in under three seconds.

HOW TO DRAW: A VAMPIRE

Begin with a tall, slender oval for the body. Add a sharp, angular face with a widow's peak. Draw slicked-back hair and pointy ears. Don't forget the fangs! Add a cape flowing behind the vampire and give them a mysterious gaze. Watch out for those fangs!

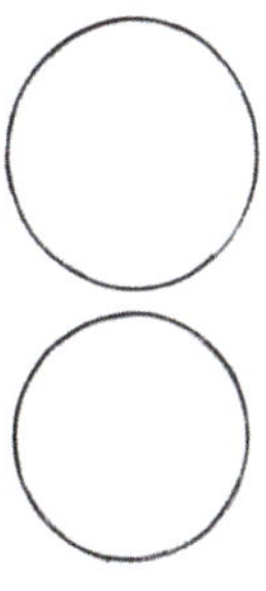
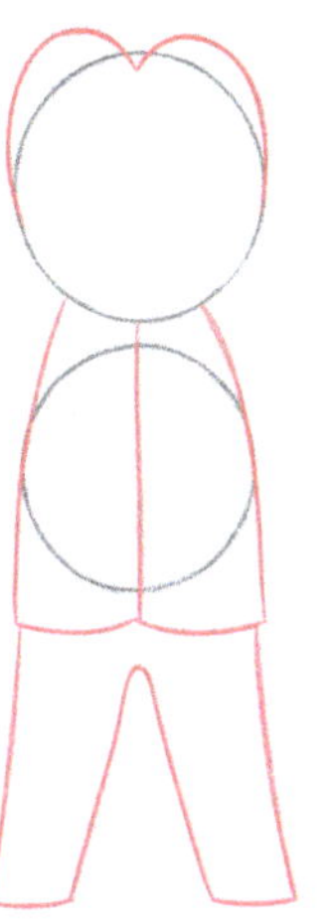

Joke

What's the difference between a dog and a crocodile?

Answer: The dog's bark is worst than his bite!

HOW TO DRAW: A WEREWOLF

Start with a large oval for the body. Add a wolf-like head with pointy ears. Draw a muscular body and strong, hairy legs. Don't forget the sharp claws! Give your werewolf a ferocious expression and let its wild side shine. Howl at the moon like a werewolf!

YOUR TURN!

Fun Fact

Cheetahs are the world's fastest land animals over short distances, capable of reaching speeds of up to 64 miles per hour in under three seconds.

HOW TO DRAW: A YETI

Let's venture into the snowy mountains and draw a mighty Yeti! Begin with a large, hulking figure. Add broad shoulders and long arms with big hands. Draw shaggy fur all over the body. Give your Yeti a friendly face and a mischievous smile. Leave footprints in the snow like a Yeti!

YOUR TURN!

HOW TO DRAW: NATURE AND LANDSCAPES

It's time to dive into the fascinating world of domestic animals. These furry friends bring joy and companionship to our lives, and we're going to learn how to draw them step-by-step. Get your pencils ready, and let's embark on an artistic adventure with some adorable domestic animals!

INDEX

HOW TO DRAW: GRASS

Let's create a lush field of grass! Begin with short, curvy lines that represent the blades of grass. Draw them in various heights and angles to give a sense of depth. Imagine the gentle sway of the grass in the wind!

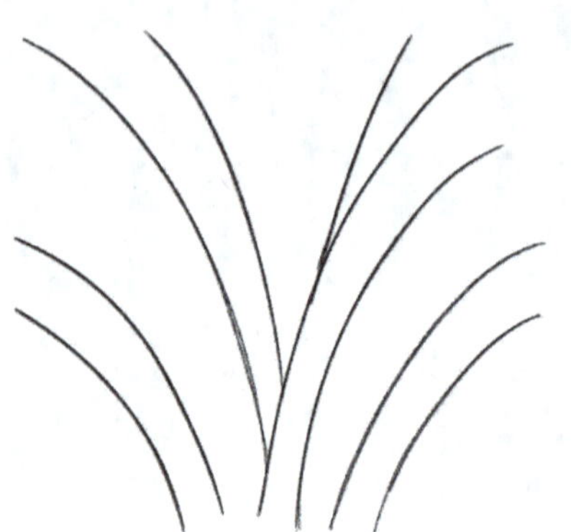

EXPERIMENT WITH DIFFERENT STYLES

YOUR TURN!

HOW TO DRAW: FLOWERS

Start with a big circle for the center of the flower. Add long, curved petals around the circle, radiating outward like sunrays. Draw a stem and leaves at the bottom.

YOUR TURN!

HOW TO DRAW: TREES

Start by drawing a vertical line for the trunk. Add branches that spread out like arms reaching for the sky. Draw leaves or needles on the branches. Remember, trees come in various shapes and sizes, so let your creativity guide you. Imagine the breeze rustling through the leaves!

EXPERIMENT WITH DIFFERENT STYLES

YOUR TURN!

HOW TO DRAW: CACTI

Let's draw a spiky friend from the desert! Begin with a vertical oval shape for the body. Add short, thick spikes all around. Draw a cluster of small flowers on top for a touch of desert charm. Watch out for those prickly thorns!

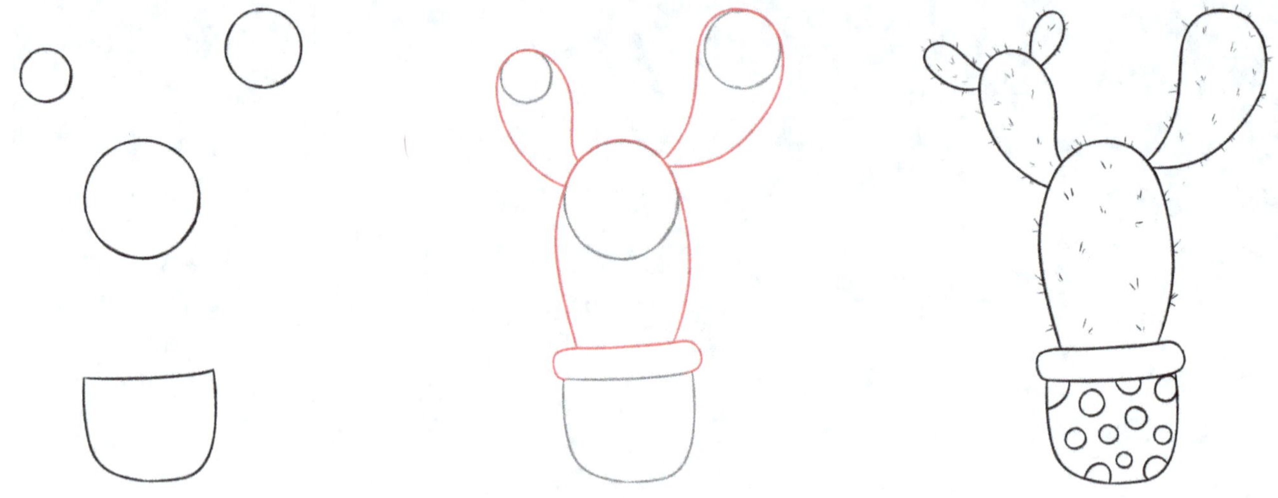

EXPERIMENT WITH DIFFERENT STYLES

YOUR TURN!

HOW TO DRAW: MUSHROOMS

Start with a round shape for the mushroom cap. Add a short, thick stem below. Draw small dots or lines on the cap for texture. Let your mushroom come alive with whimsical colors. Perhaps a fairy will come to visit!

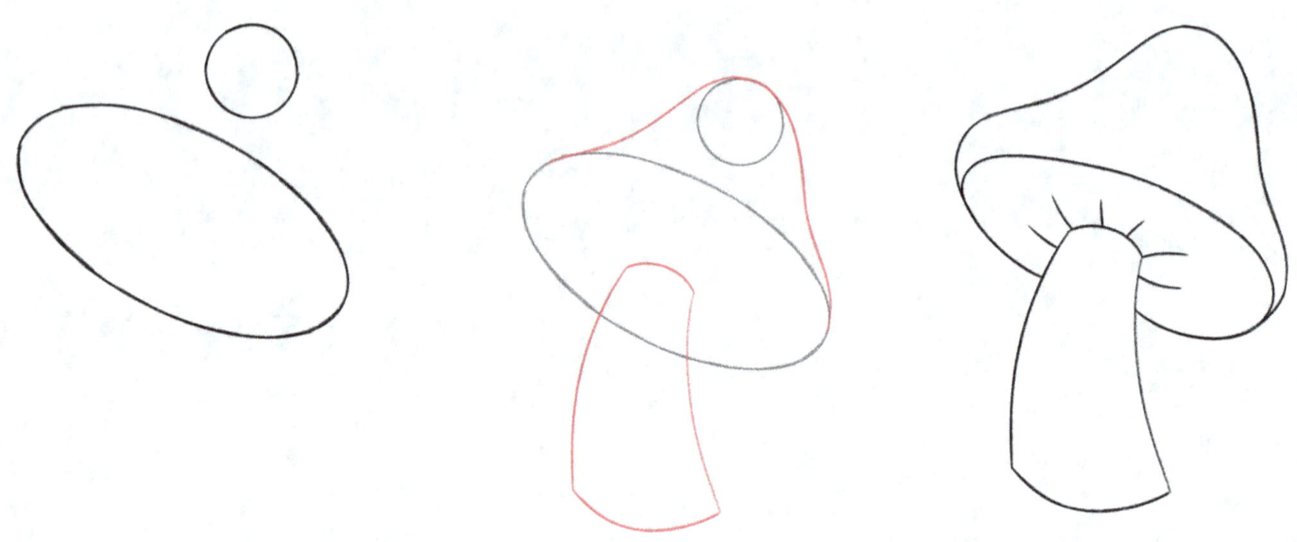

EXPERIMENT WITH DIFFERENT STYLES

YOUR TURN!

HOW TO DRAW: LEAVES

Start with a curvy line for the center vein of the leaf. Add elongated shapes on both sides, creating the leaf's form. Draw smaller veins branching out from the center vein. You can draw different types of leaves, like oak, maple, or heart-shaped leaves. Celebrate the beauty of autumn!

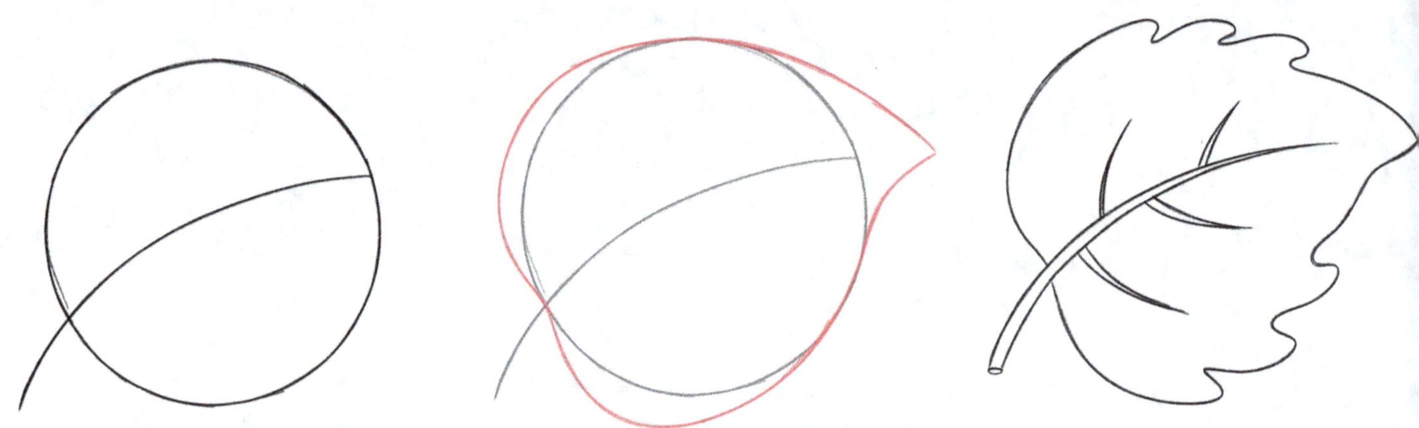

EXPERIMENT WITH DIFFERENT STYLES

YOUR TURN!

HOW TO DRAW: GEMS

Let's add some sparkle to our artwork with dazzling gems! Begin by drawing a simple geometric shape, such as a diamond, oval, or heart, to represent the gem's base. Add facets to the shape by drawing diagonal lines or curves across its surface. This will give the gem a multifaceted appearance. a

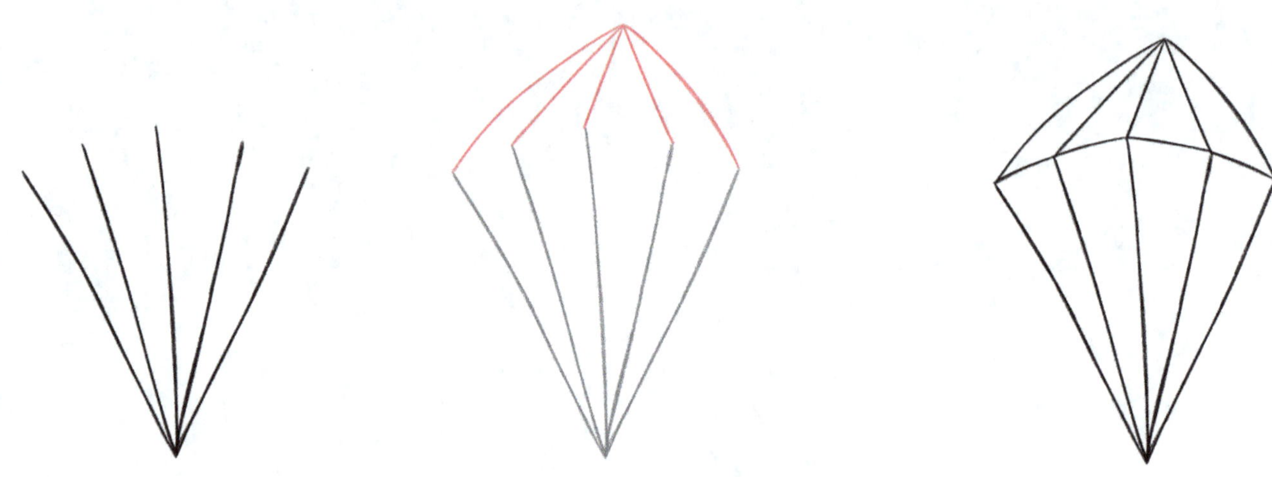

EXPERIMENT WITH DIFFERENT STYLES

YOUR TURN!

HOW TO DRAW: LANDSCAPES

Let's create a picturesque landscape that captures the beauty of nature! Start by drawing a horizontal line near the bottom of your paper to represent the horizon. Now use the previous lessons to add trees, scattered across the landscape, a winding path or river that leads into the distance, and a bright sun, fluffy clouds, or even a colorful sunset to complete the scene. Don't forget to add details like flowers, birds, or a cozy cottage to make your landscape come alive.

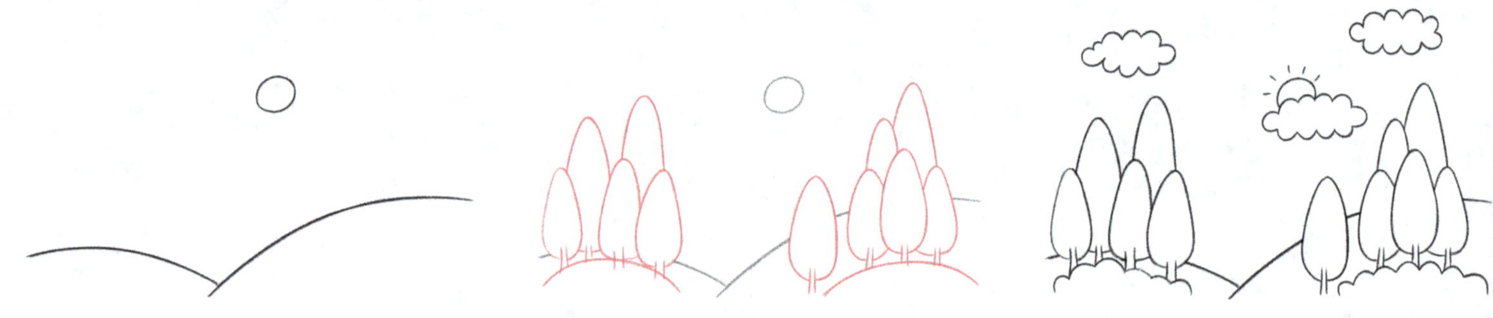

EXPERIMENT WITH DIFFERENT STYLES

YOUR TURN!

HOW TO DRAW: EVERYDAY OBJECTS

In this chapter, we will explore the art of drawing things we encounter in our daily lives. Get ready to bring these objects to life on your paper with your creative skills. So, grab your pencils and let's embark on an imaginative journey filled with familiar items that make our world colorful and exciting!

INDEX

HOW TO DRAW: KEYS

Begin by drawing a simple rectangle shape. Add a curved line at the top to create the key's bow. Draw a straight line extending from the bottom of the rectangle to form the key's blade. You can even add patterns or designs to your key to make it unique.

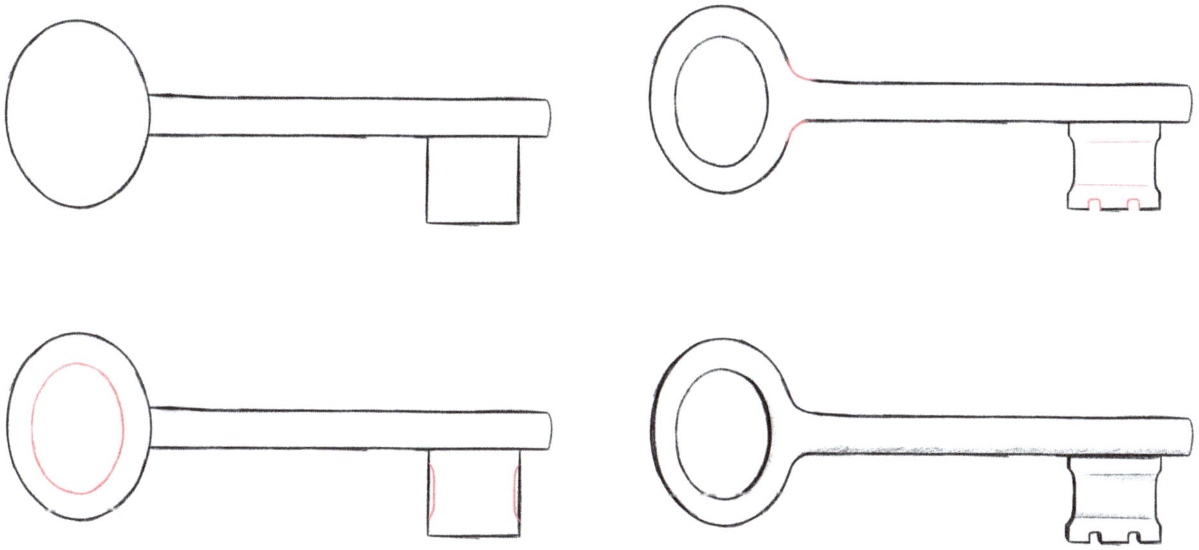

EXPERIMENT WITH DIFFERENT STYLES

HOW TO DRAW: CLOCKS

Start by drawing a circle to represent the clock face. Add numbers around the circle to mark the hours. Draw two hands - a shorter one for the hours and a longer one for the minutes. You can even add details like ticks or a pendulum if you like.

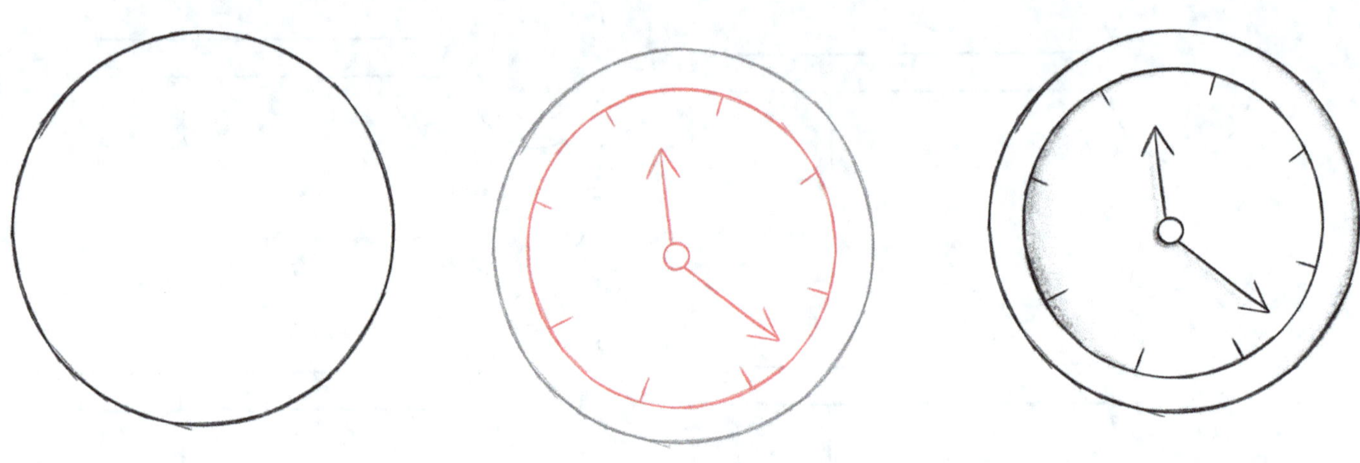

EXPERIMENT WITH DIFFERENT STYLES

HOW TO DRAW: LIGHT BULBS

Begin by drawing a round shape for the bulb. Add a curved line at the bottom for the base. Draw a few lines inside the bulb to represent the filament. You can even add rays or sparkles to show the glow.

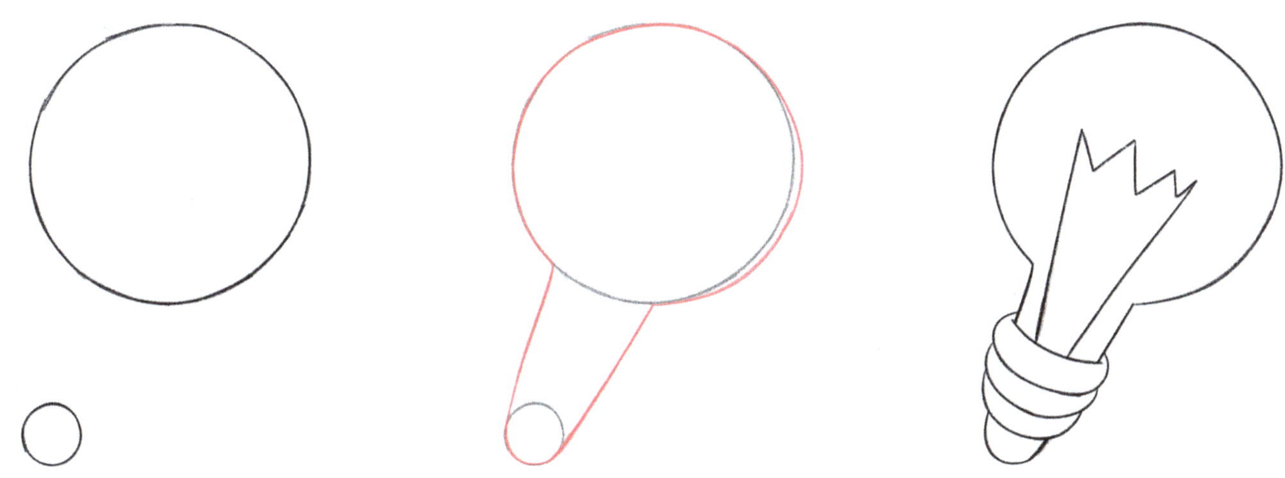

EXPERIMENT WITH DIFFERENT STYLES

HOW TO DRAW: BUTTONS

Start by drawing a small circle or any shape you like for the button's face. Add holes or a design in the center. You can even draw a thread attached to the button.

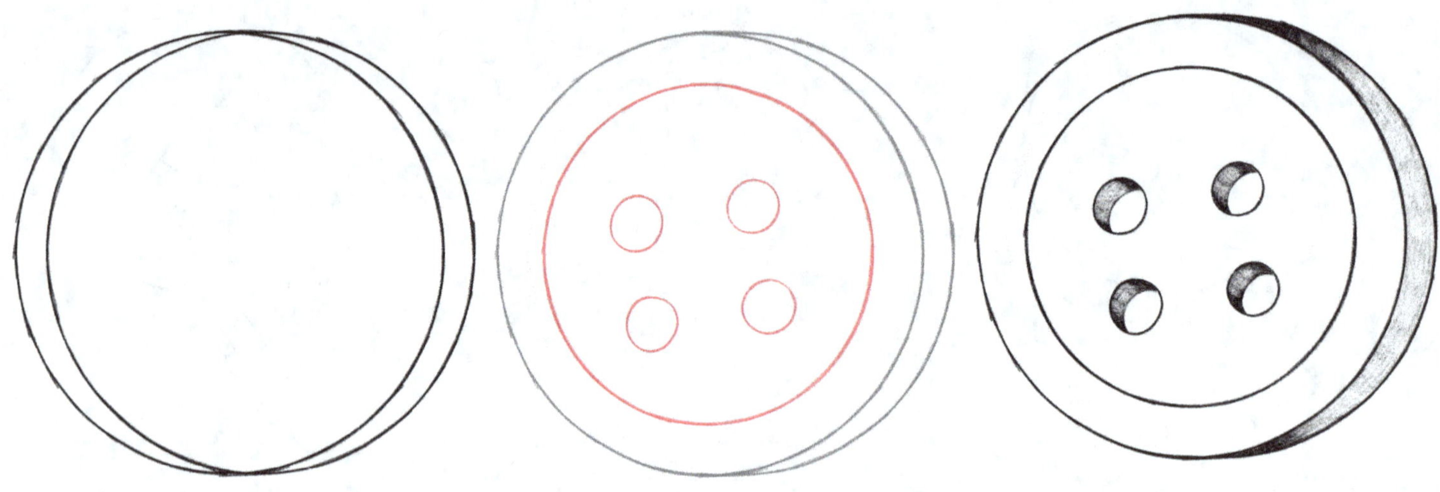

EXPERIMENT WITH DIFFERENT STYLES

HOW TO DRAW: MAGNETS

Begin by drawing a rectangular shape for the magnet's body. Add a curved shape at one end to represent the magnet's pole. Draw lines or arrows to indicate the magnetic field. You can even add a few paperclips or small metal objects nearby, showing their magnetic bond.

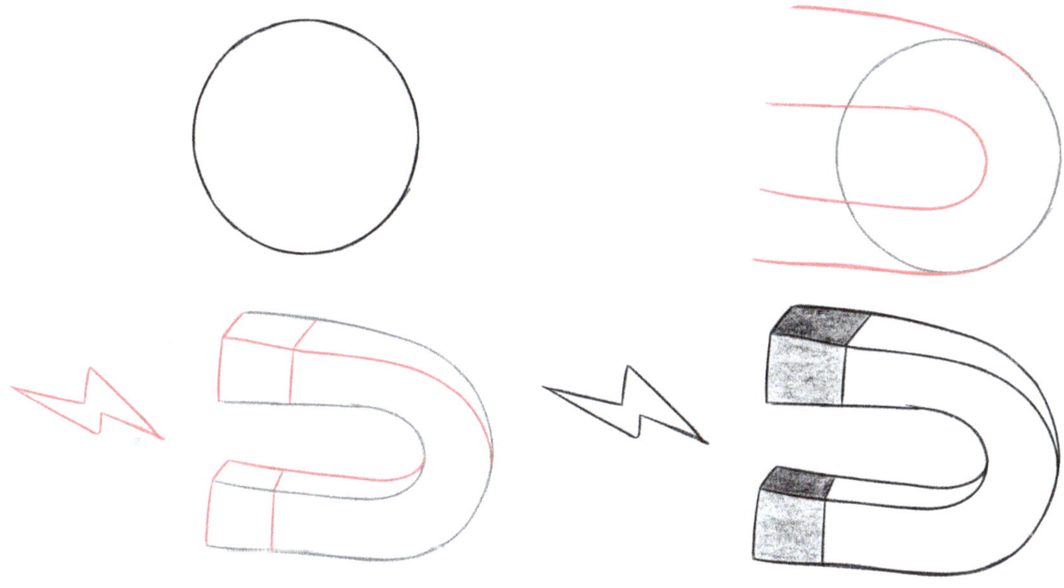

WITH DIFFERENT STYLES

HOW TO DRAW: PENS

Start by drawing a straight line for the pen's body. Add a small rectangle or oval shape at one end for the pen's cap. Draw a cylindrical shape at the other end for the pen tip. You can even add a clip or some details to make it unique.

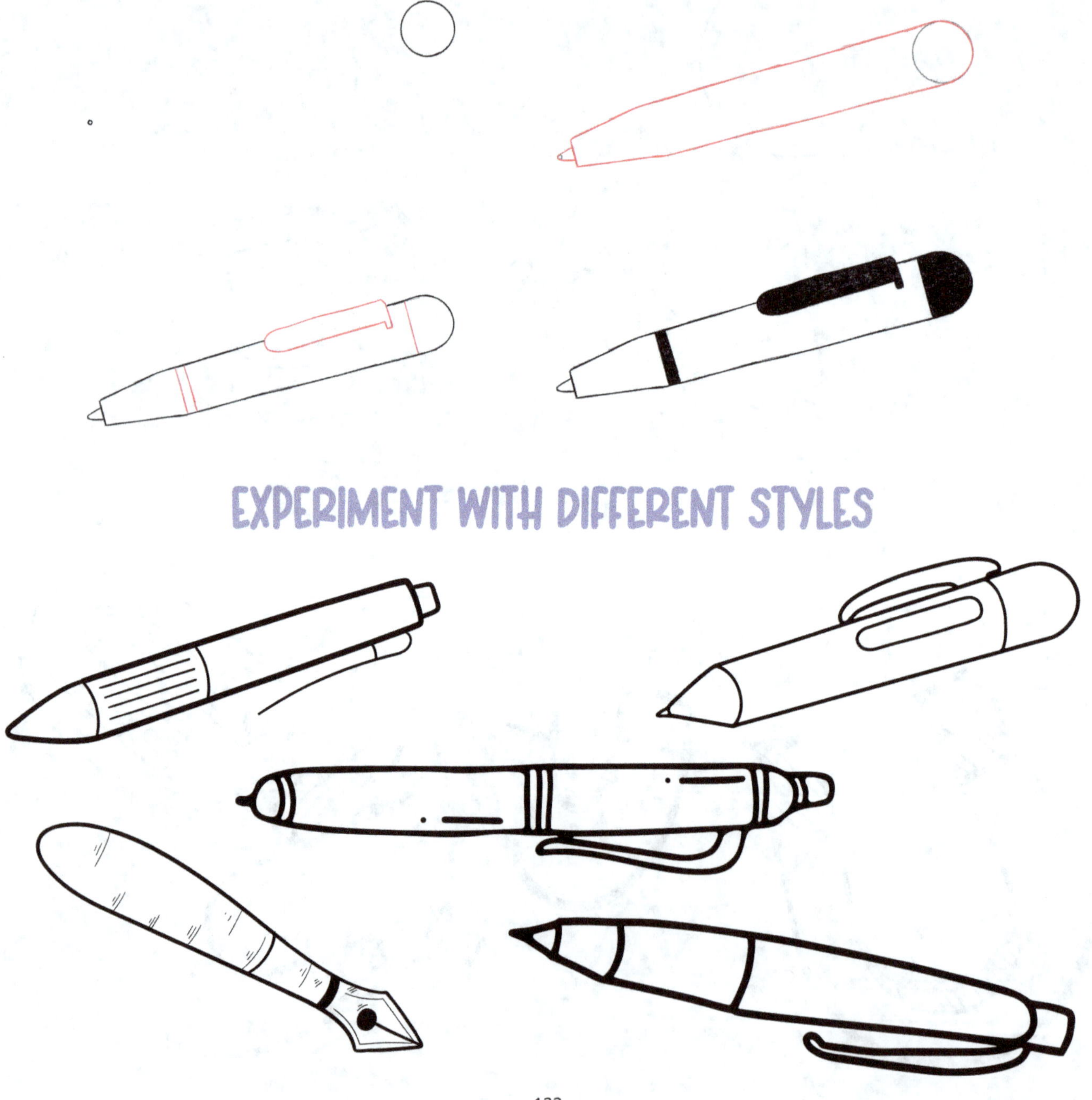

HOW TO DRAW: GLASSES

Begin by drawing two oval shapes for the lenses. Connect the lenses with a curved line for the bridge. Add two curved lines on each side for the arms. You can also draw patterns or reflections on the lenses.

EXPERIMENT WITH DIFFERENT STYLES

HOW TO DRAW: MUGS

Begin by drawing a curved line for the top rim of the mug. Add the sides with straight lines that converge towards the bottom. Draw a handle on one side to complete the mug. Don't forget to add some decorations or patterns to make it unique.

EXPERIMENT WITH DIFFERENT STYLES

HOW TO DRAW: HAIRBRUSHES

Begin by drawing a rectangular shape for the brush body. Add a curved or zigzag line at the top to represent the bristles. Draw a handle at the bottom.

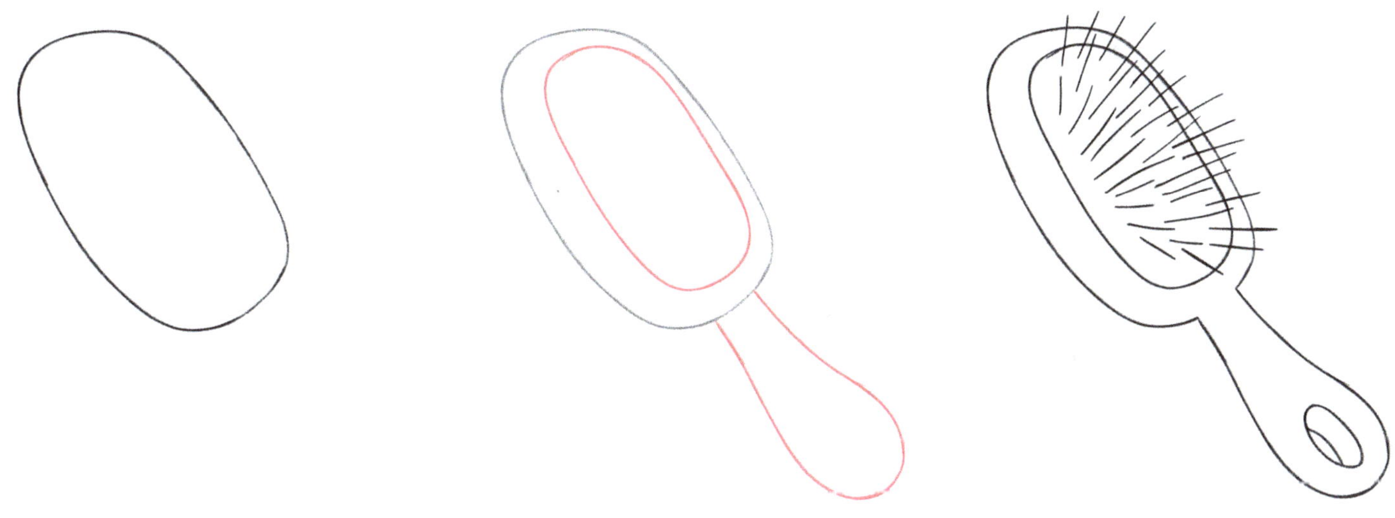

EXPERIMENT WITH DIFFERENT STYLES

HOW TO DRAW: CELLPHONES

Begin by drawing a rectangle with rounded corners for the screen. Add a smaller rectangle at the bottom for the home button. Draw a few buttons or icons on the screen to represent different apps.

EXPERIMENT WITH DIFFERENT STYLES

HOW TO DRAW: CARS

Begin by drawing a rectangular shape for the car body. Add circles or ellipses for the wheels. Draw a curved line on top for the windshield. Add details like windows, headlights, and even some patterns or designs.

EXPERIMENT WITH DIFFERENT STYLES

HOW TO DRAW: BUSES

Start by drawing a long, rectangular shape for the bus body. Add wheels at the bottom with circles or ellipses. Draw windows along the length of the bus. Don't forget the front windshield and the headlights. You can even draw some passengers peering out of the windows.

EXPERIMENT WITH DIFFERENT STYLES

HOW TO DRAW: PLANES

Start by drawing a long, oval shape for the airplane body. Add wings on each side with curved lines. Draw a tail at the back. Don't forget the cockpit windows and the engines under the wings.

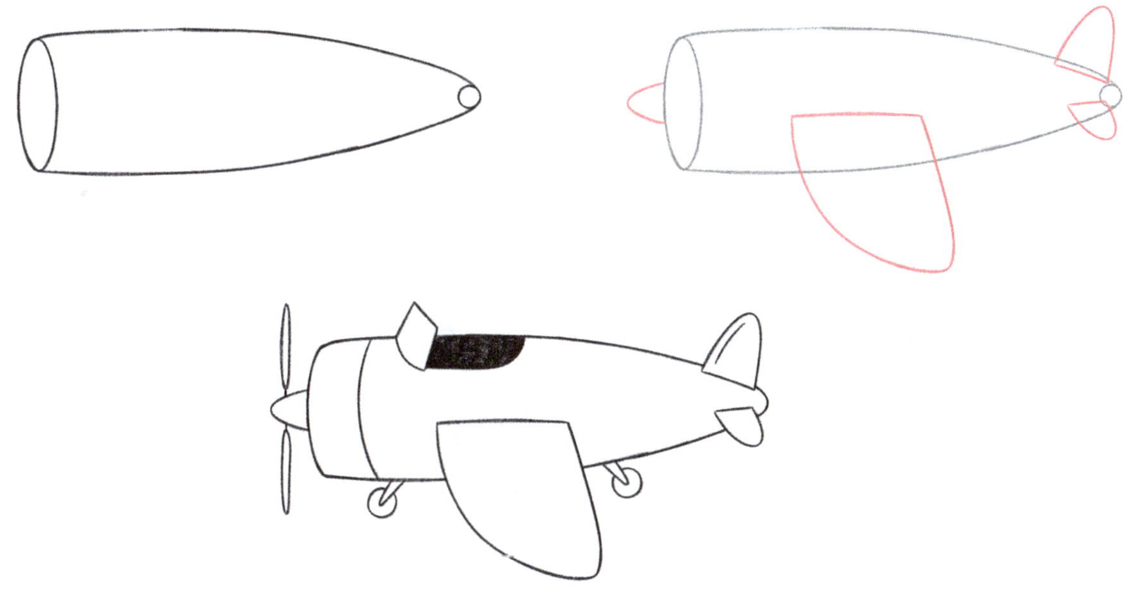

EXPERIMENT WITH DIFFERENT STYLES

HOW TO DRAW: MOTORCYCLES

Start by drawing two circles for the wheels. Connect them with a curved line for the frame. Add a smaller circle for the headlight. Draw handlebars and a seat. Don't forget the exhaust pipe at the back.

EXPERIMENT WITH DIFFERENT STYLES

HOW TO DRAW: TRAINS

Begin by drawing a long, rectangular shape for the train body. Add wheels along the length with circles or ellipses. Draw windows and a front windshield for the engine. Connect the train cars with smaller rectangles. Don't forget the smoke coming out of the engine's chimney.

EXPERIMENT WITH DIFFERENT STYLES

HOW TO DRAW: APPLES

Begin by drawing a round shape for the apple's body. Add a small leaf at the top. Draw a curved line across the apple to represent its shine. You can even add a bite mark or some seeds inside.

EXPERIMENT WITH DIFFERENT STYLES

HOW TO DRAW: PIZZA

Start by drawing a triangular shape for the pizza slice. Add cheese and your favorite toppings - pepperoni, mushrooms, or bell peppers. Draw some tomato sauce dripping from the toppings. You can even add a few bubbles of cheese.

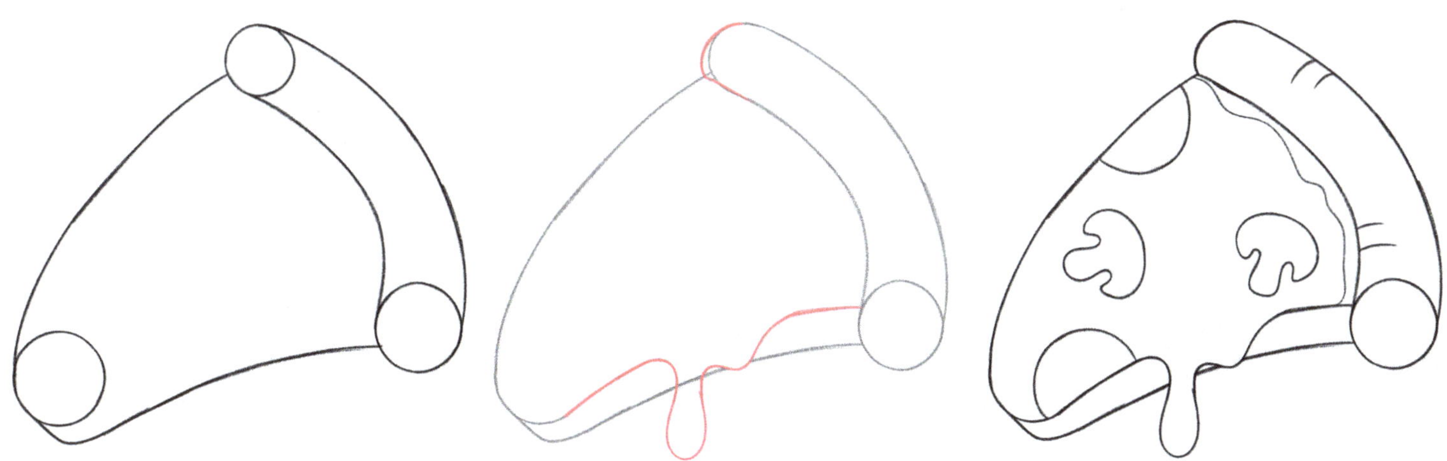

EXPERIMENT WITH DIFFERENT STYLES

HOW TO DRAW: ICECREAM

Begin by drawing a triangular shape for the cone. Add a swirl shape on top for the ice cream scoop. Draw lines or curves to create the texture of the ice cream. You can also add sprinkles or a cherry on top.

EXPERIMENT WITH DIFFERENT STYLES

HOW TO DRAW: HAMBURGERS

Start by drawing two parallel lines for the burger buns. Add a circular shape for the patty in between. Draw cheese, lettuce, tomatoes, and other toppings. Don't forget to add a layer of ketchup or mustard, and draw sesame seeds on the bun.

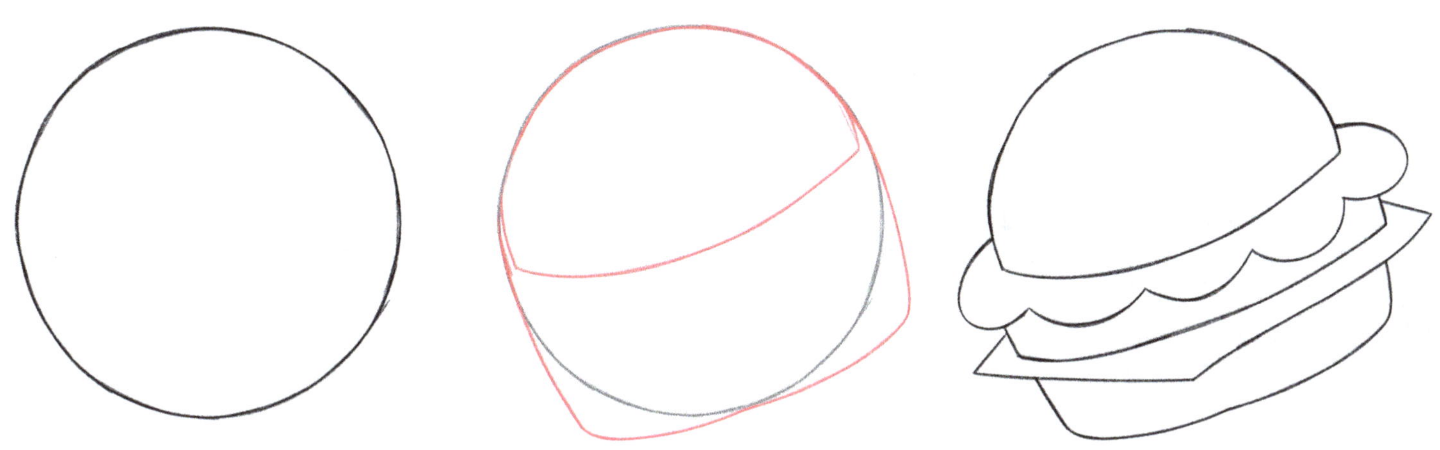

EXPERIMENT WITH DIFFERENT STYLES

HOW TO DRAW: CUPCAKES

Begin by drawing a round shape for the cupcake's base. Add a smaller circle on top for the frosting. Draw lines or swirls to create the texture of the frosting. Add a cherry or sprinkles for extra decoration.

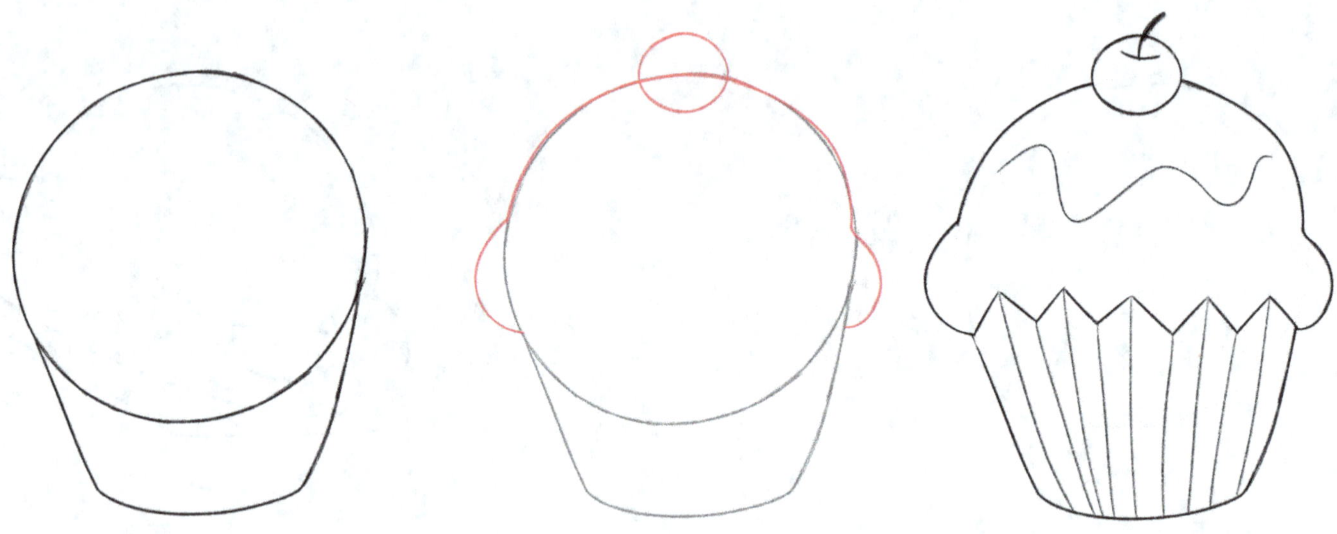

EXPERIMENT WITH DIFFERENT STYLES

CREATING YOUR OWN ARTWORK

Welcome to the magical world of creating your very own artwork! In this chapter, we will explore how to find inspiration and let your imagination soar. Get ready to embark on a creative journey filled with ideas, joy, and self-expression!

OBSERVE THE WORLD AROUND YOU

Inspiration is everywhere! Take a moment to observe the world around you. Look at the beauty of nature, the shapes and colors of objects, the expressions on people's faces, or even the patterns in everyday items. Let these observations spark your imagination and become the starting point for your artwork.

EXPLORE YOUR INTERESTS

Think about the things you love and enjoy. Do you have a favorite animal, hobby, or place? Maybe you're fascinated by outer space or dream of becoming a superhero. Whatever it is, let your passions and interests inspire your artwork. Draw what makes you happy and what excites your imagination.

DIVE INTO BOOKS AND STORIES

Books are like portals to new worlds. Read stories, fairy tales, and adventures that captivate your imagination. Imagine yourself as the hero of the story or create artwork based on your favorite characters. Let the words on the pages transport you to new realms of creativity.

VISIT MUSEUMS AND GALLERIES

Museums and art galleries are treasure troves of inspiration. Take a trip to a local museum or explore art exhibitions online. Observe the colors, brushstrokes, and emotions captured in different artworks. Allow these experiences to inspire your own artistic style and ideas.

EXPERIMENT WITH DIFFERENT MATERIALS

Don't limit yourself to just one art medium. Try different materials like paints, markers, clay, or collage. Each medium offers unique possibilities for creativity. Let your curiosity guide you and experiment with different techniques and textures.

LET YOUR IMAGINATION RUN WILD

Sometimes the best inspiration comes from within. Close your eyes, take a deep breath, and let your imagination run wild. Visualize a world of magic, invent new creatures, or imagine yourself in extraordinary places. Then, put pen to paper and bring your imagination to life through your artwork.

COLLABORATE AND SHARE

Art is even more enjoyable when shared with others. Collaborate with friends or family members on art projects. Exchange ideas, combine your skills, and create collaborative artwork. Sharing your artwork with others can also inspire new ideas and perspectives.

EMBRACE MISTAKES AND LEARN

Remember, art is all about self-expression and exploration. Don't be afraid to make mistakes or try new things. Mistakes can lead to unexpected discoveries and open doors to new artistic possibilities. Embrace the learning process and allow yourself to grow as an artist.

TRUST YOUR INSTINCTS

When creating your own artwork, trust your instincts and follow your heart. There are no right or wrong answers in art. Express yourself freely and let your artwork reflect your unique thoughts, emotions, and personality.

Creating artwork is a journey of self-discovery and joy. Embrace the process, enjoy each stroke of the brush or pencil, and allow yourself to get lost in the flow of creativity. The journey itself is just as important as the final artwork.

Find inspiration in the world around you, explore your interests, and let your imagination guide your artwork. Create with joy, passion, and an open heart, and watch as your creativity blossoms into beautiful works of art.

HAPPY CREATING!

Congratulations, young artist! You've reached the end of this incredible drawing adventure. Throughout this book, you've learned so many valuable lessons, discovered new techniques, and let your imagination run wild. Now it's time to wrap up this artistic journey and embrace the limitless possibilities that lie ahead.

As you reflect on your progress, you'll notice how much you've grown and improved as an artist. From your first drawings to your latest creations, celebrate your achievements and be proud of your artistic journey.

Embrace your unique style that has developed as you've explored different subjects, techniques, and mediums. Your style is what makes your artwork special and authentic. Allow your unique voice to shine through in every stroke of the brush or pencil.

Remember that art is a never-ending adventure. There's always something new to learn and explore. Continue seeking inspiration, experimenting with different techniques, and challenging yourself to grow as an artist. The journey of artistic discovery has just begun!

Share your artwork with the world. Display it proudly, participate in art exhibitions, or even create your own online gallery. Let your art be a source of joy and inspiration for others. Art has the power to connect and inspire, so let your creations spread happiness far and wide.

Stay curious and open-minded. The world is full of wonders and inspiration. Explore different art forms, visit exhibitions, and learn about artists from different cultures and backgrounds. Let these experiences broaden your artistic horizons.

Practice, practice, practice. Set aside time regularly to draw and create. The more you practice, the more your skills will grow and evolve. Whether it's a few minutes each day or dedicated art sessions, make drawing a part of your life.

In the face of challenges, stay positive and embrace them as opportunities to learn and grow. Art, like life, can sometimes have difficulties. Don't let them discourage you. Instead, remember that every mistake is a stepping stone to improvement.

Use your artistic talents to spread kindness. Art has the power to uplift, inspire, and bring joy. Create artwork that brightens someone's day, whether it's a heartfelt greeting card, a mural in your community, or a piece of art for a charity event. Let your art make a difference.

Above all, never forget the joy of creating. Let your art be a source of happiness and self-expression. Get lost in the process, savor every stroke, and allow your imagination to roam freely. Creating art is a gift that brings immense joy to both the artist and those who experience it.

This book marks the end of a chapter, but it's only the beginning of your artistic journey. Keep exploring, keep learning, and keep creating. Let your art evolve and grow as you do. The possibilities are endless, and the world eagerly awaits your next masterpiece.

Thank you for joining us on this artistic adventure. You are a talented artist with a vibrant imagination and a boundless creative spirit. Remember, the artist within you is always there, ready to unleash its magic. So, continue to nurture your artistic passion, and may your artistic journey be filled with endless inspiration and fulfillment.

Keep creating, young artist, and let your art change the world!